BATHROOM SCIENCE

70 FUN AND WACKY SCIENCE EXPERIMENTS

Christine Taylor-Butler

PORTABLE
PRESS

Portable Press/The Bathroom Readers' Institute
An imprint of Printers Row Publishing Group
10350 Barnes Canyon Road, Suite 100, San Diego, CA 92121
www.portablepress.com
e-mail: mail@bathroomreader.com

Printers Row Publishing Group is a division of Readerlink Distribution Services, LLC. The Portable Press name and logo is a trademark of Readerlink Distribution Services, LLC.

All correspondence concerning the content of this book should be addressed to Portable Press, Editorial Department, at the above address.

Cover and interior design by Tom Deja/Bossman Graphics

Thank You

Gordon Javna	Kim T. Griswell
Brian Boone	Dan Mansfield
Trina Janssen	Melinda Allman
Jay Newman	Thomas Edison

Library of Congress Cataloging-in-Publication Data

Names: Taylor-Butler, Christine.
Title: Bathroom science : 70 fun and wacky science experiments
Description: San Diego, CA : Portable Press, 2016. | Audience: Age 8+.?
Identifiers: LCCN 2016005031 | ISBN 9781626865877 (pbk., concealed spiral)
Subjects: LCSH: Science--Experiments--Juvenile literature. |
  Science--Miscellanea--Juvenile literature.
Classification: LCC Q164 .T39 2016 | DDC 507.8--dc23

Printed in China
First Printing
20 19 18 17 16   1 2 3 4 5

THE EXPERIMENTS

NOTE: Experiments listed in red involve sharp objects, bleach, fire, or other things you shouldn't handle on your own. Get an adult to help you with these.

IT'S ALIVE!

Science: It's literally how the world and everything in it works. Its principles affect the air, the water, the ground, and our bodies. And with *Bathroom Science* you can discover the science that's all around you by conducting 70 simple, easy-to-follow experiments, using items that are also all around you.

We recommend the bathroom for doing these experiments because you've got a great scientific tool chest in there: You can make the room hot or cold with a shower, there's plenty of water at the ready, and a there's a sink or a tub to catch anything messy. (By the way, you *will* make a mess. Guaranteed!) Who knew the bathroom was so educational? There are way more scientific questions that can be answered in that little room than just, "Why does shampoo hurt my eyes?"

IMPORTANT NOTE: Some of these experiments will require adult supervision or assistance. (Hey, nobody ever said unlocking the secrets of the universe would be easy.) When objects like a hammer, matches, or bleach are involved, it's best to leave those steps to a grown-up in the house. The ones that require an adult hand are listed on the table of contents in red. (Also, did the promise of fire and chemicals make you want to do these experiments just a *little* bit more? Excellent!)

A very special thank you to Rachel and Claire, our 12-year-old *Bathroom Science* lab technicians who tested all of these experiments for maximum safety, fun, and "wow" factor.

So grab your equipment, head into the bathroom, and get to it!

THE TOILET VOLCANO

FORGET ABOUT USING A SCRUB BRUSH TO CLEAN YOUR TOILET. MAKE THE THRONE ERUPT ITSELF CLEAN!

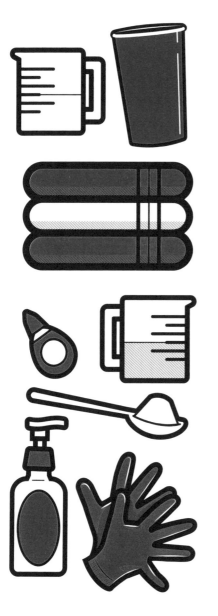

WHAT YOU NEED

2 tablespoons baking soda
1 cup vinegar
1 cup warm water
Liquid soap
Disposable plastic cup
Red food coloring
Latex or rubber gloves
Toilet
Lots of old towels

HOW TO DO IT

1. Have an adult turn off the water to the toilet, and flush it until all the water drains out.
2. Put towels around the toilet to catch any potential spills, and put on the rubber gloves.
3. In the plastic cup, mix the warm water with a few drops of liquid soap. Then add a few drops of red food coloring.
4. Add the baking soda.
5. Carefully place the cup into the empty toilet bowl.
6. Pour the vinegar inside the cup.
7. Stand back!

WHAT'S GOING ON HERE?

The baking soda and vinegar erupt because of an *acid-base reaction*. Acetic acid (vinegar) reacts with *sodium bicarbonate* (baking soda). This creates carbon dioxide gas. The gas reacts with the remaining liquid to create the fizzing and bubbling effect. The liquid soap helps increase the amount of foam produced. (This experiment may also help clean and sanitize your toilet without chemicals—baking soda and vinegar are effective, safe ingredients in lots of cleaning supplies.)

THE GLOWING GOO

NEED A BATHROOM NIGHT-LIGHT? THIS COULD DO THE TRICK.

WHAT YOU NEED

1 cup hot water
1 cup Epsom salt
1 cup school glue
Glow-in-the-dark paint
Paper bowl

HOW TO DO IT

1. Pour the water into the bowl and add the Epsom salt. Rapidly stir until it starts to dissolve.
2. Stir in the glue until smooth.
3. Stir in about three tablespoons of glow-in-the-dark paint.
4. Continue stirring until solid.
5. Turn off the lights!

WHAT'S GOING ON HERE?

The glue (scientific name: *polyvinyl acetate resin*) is a polymer, which means "many units." The combination of Epsom salt, glue, and water sets up a chemical reaction to form a compound that is solid. The Epsom salt binds to the glue to make the glue's polymer strands stronger, but still allows it to stretch. As for the glow, the paint contains phosphorous pigments that are activated when exposed to light.

SLIME TIME

GOOD SLIME IS SO HARD TO FIND THESE DAYS.
YOU MIGHT AS WELL JUST MAKE YOUR OWN.

WHAT YOU NEED

2 bowls
1/2 cup school glue
1-1/2 cups water
Food coloring
1 teaspoon borax
Resealable plastic sandwich bag

HOW TO DO IT

1. Pour the glue and half a cup of water into a bowl. Stir.
2. Add a few drops of food coloring. (Green is the most slimelike, but you can use any color you want. Or even more than one!)
3. In a second bowl, add the borax to the rest of the water. Stir until the borax is completely dissolved.
4. Slowly pour the colored glue mixture into the borax mixture, and stir the mixing concoctions as you do it.

5. While there may be a little bit of extra water hanging around, the result should be a semisolid hunk of slimy green goop. Pull it out of the bowl, and pull and squish your new slime! (To save the slime for future slime-requiring activities, store it in a resealable plastic sandwich bag.)

WHAT'S GOING ON HERE?

A *compound* is formed by combining two or more substances into a mixture that can't easily be separated. Glue + borax + water = compound. Additionally, glue is a *polymer*, which means it contains individual molecules that can slide past each other while still holding together as a substance. When borax bonds with water, electrically charged molecules called *ions* form. Those, in turn, more tightly link the polymer molecules in the glue. The final effect of all of this: a slimy, rubbery substance.

IT'S SNOT MUCH TROUBLE

WHY WOULD YOU WANT TO MAKE ARTIFICIAL SNOT? WHO NOSE WHY?

WHAT YOU NEED

1/2 cup boiling water

3 teaspoons unflavored gelatin

Medium bowl

Green food coloring (If you don't have unflavored gelatin, you can use lime gelatin, and skip the food coloring.)

1/2 cup corn syrup

Fork

HOW TO DO IT

1. After you have an adult boil some water for you, have them measure and pour 1/2 cup into the bowl.
2. Carefully stir in the gelatin until it dissolves, and then add a few drops of the green food coloring. (If you're going with the lime gelatin, just stir that in now.)
3. Now, mix in the corn syrup. Stir until it's slimy, roughly the consistency of the stuff that flies out of your nose when you've got a cold. (Gesundheit!)

4. Use the fork to lift the concoction onto, say, a handkerchief, your little brother's arm, etc.

WHAT'S GOING ON HERE?

The gelatin contains protein and sugars. You know what else contains protein and sugars? The mucus in your nose, otherwise known as snot. When gelatin cools and bonds with water molecules, it usually forms a solid. But when the corn syrup binds to the gelatin, it helps it stay a thick liquid, allowing molecules to slide over each other. That makes it a polymer, like the glue in "Slime Time." (See page 10.)

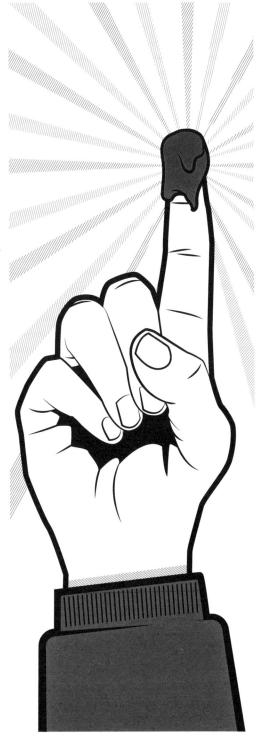

STRING THEORY

DO YOU HAVE TROUBLE POURING THINGS WITHOUT SPILLING?
THEN PAY ATTENTION.

WHAT YOU NEED

2 water glasses
2 feet of cotton string
Water

HOW TO DO IT

1. Fill one glass halfway with water, and place in the sink.
2. Put the whole string in the water and allow it to soak thoroughly.
3. Pull out the string, leaving one end in the water.
4. Hold the other end of the string over the empty glass.
5. Lift the glass of water until it's higher than the empty glass. Hold the top string tightly to the rim of the glass while you lift. You may need to hold both ends of string to their cups. (And make sure the string between the two glasses is stretched tight.)
6. Slowly tip the water glass so the water travels down the string into the empty glass.

WHAT'S GOING ON HERE?

If you pour slowly enough, the water will stick to—and slide over—the water molecules in the wet string, allowing it to flow into the cup. The string can only hold so much water at a time, which is why a slow speed is necessary. If you pour too fast, the weight of the water will simply cause it to flow toward the ground.

DECORATING, CAVEMAN STYLE

MAKE SOME STALACTITES AND STALAGMITES TO GIVE YOUR
BATHROOM SOME MUCH-NEEDED "CAVE APPEAL."

WHAT YOU NEED

6 pieces of yarn or string,
   each 2 feet long
Box of Epsom salt
4 metal washers
4 small water glasses
Warm water
Shallow pan

HOW TO DO IT

1. Cut three pieces of yarn that are
   each two feet long.
2. Braid the pieces of yarn together.
3. Tie a washer onto each end of
   the braids.
4. Fill each glass two-thirds full
   with water.
5. Pour Epsom salt into each glass
   until it dissolves.
6. Place the glasses in the pan next
   to a sunny window.
7. Place one end of a braid into
   each cup.

8. Push the glasses together so the yarn between them hangs down to form a valley.
9. Check back in a few days. What do you see on the string? In the pan?

WHAT'S GOING ON HERE?

Stalactites and *stalagmites* form when water seeps through soft limestone walls. The minerals dissolve and travel with the water. When the water evaporates, the minerals remain behind. The same is happening with your Epsom salt solution. Stalactites stick to the yarn, while stalagmites form from the water that dripped into the pan.

HOW TO MAKE A FLOWER SWEAT

DID YOU KNOW THAT PLANTS SWEAT, TOO? THEY JUST DON'T HAVE TO TAKE A SHOWER WHEN THEY DO.

WHAT YOU NEED

White flowers with leaves
Resealable plastic sandwich bags
Rubber band
Tall water glass
Scissors
Sunny window

HOW TO DO IT

1. Fill the glass halfway with water.
2. Cut 1/2 inch from the bottom of the stem, at a slight angle.
3. Immediately place the flower in the glass of water.
4. Cover the head(s) of the flower and a few leaves with the plastic bag.
5. Seal the bag, making sure air is trapped inside. Use the rubber band to secure the bag and make sure no air can escape.
6. Place the flower and glass near a sunny window.
7. Let it sit for 24 hours. What happens inside the bag?

WHAT'S GOING ON HERE?

Flowers need water to grow and thrive. A flower can pull water up through its stem, bringing minerals and nutrients with it. But only 10 percent of the water drawn through the stem is absorbed by the plant. So where does the rest of the water go? Flowers and leaves contain tiny pores called *stroma*. These allow the plant to breathe. Water that moves up the stem evaporates through these pores, causing more water to travel up the stem through a process called *capillary motion*. The evaporated water exits in the form of water vapor. When the water vapor touched the bag in the experiment, it cooled and condensed, forming the mist on the surface of the bag.

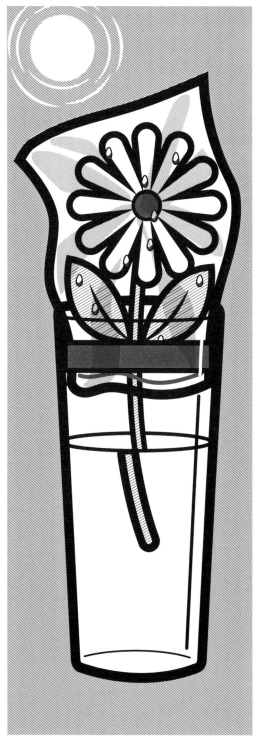

THE STRING'S THE THING

WHY FREEZE YOUR FINGERS PICKING UP ICE WHEN YOU CAN USE A STRING?

WHAT YOU NEED

Large ice cube
2 tablespoons coarse salt
String
Scissors
Tall water glass
Water

HOW TO DO IT

1. Fill the glass with water. Leave about an inch of space at the top.
2. Place the ice cube into the water. It should float.
3. Cut a piece of string about 12 inches long. Dip the string into the water until it's soaked.
4. Place one end of the string on the ice cube. Let it sit for one minute.
5. Lift up the string. Did the ice cube come up with it?
6. Re-place the string on the ice cube. Sprinkle salt onto the ice cube until the string is covered.
7. Wait one minute, then lift the string. What happens this time?

WHAT'S GOING ON HERE?

Water freezes at 32°F. When you sprinkle salt on the string and ice, this triggers an *endothermic process*. This happens when a substance takes in more energy than it gives off during a chemical reaction. In this experiment, the ice melts, breaking down the bonds between the water molecules. The salt then begins to dissolve into the water, which expends energy and cools down the water. As the temperature drops, the water refreezes in the ice and in the string, bonding them together. This allows you to pick it up.

THE BATHROOM TORNADO

IN NATURE, TORNADOES ARE DEADLY AND SHOULD
BE AVOIDED AT ALL COSTS. WE CAN MAKE
AN EXCEPTION HERE, THIS ONE TIME.

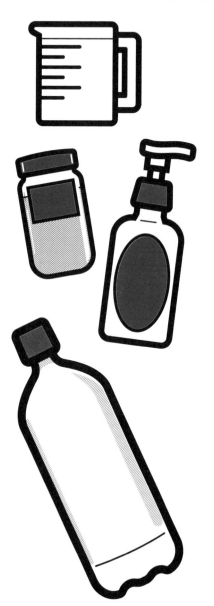

WHAT YOU NEED

Empty 2-liter soda bottle
Water
Liquid soap
Glitter

HOW TO DO IT

1. Fill the bottle with water. Leave an inch of air at the top.
2. Sprinkle in a few dashes of glitter, and then add a squirt of liquid soap.
3. Screw the cap on tightly, and turn the bottle upside down.
4. Windmill your arm while holding the lid end of the bottle tightly in your hand. Forcefully swirl the bottle in a circular motion.
5. Stop and observe.

WHAT'S GOING ON HERE?

When you swirl the bottle, it causes the water inside to spin, creating *centrifugal force*. That's an inward force that makes something travel along a curved path. As the water spins, it forms a vortex at the center. In a tornado or waterspout, the vortex is known as the eye. Eventually, the weight of the water is acted upon by gravity and the process stops.

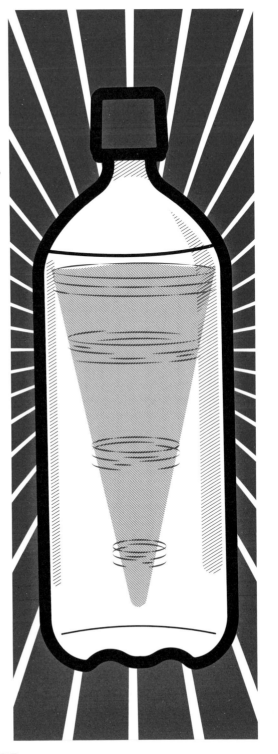

THE SCREAMING BALLOON

I SCREAM, YOU SCREAM, WE ALL SCREAM FOR...BALLOONS.

WHAT YOU NEED
Balloon
1/4-inch hex nut

HOW TO DO IT
1. Place the hex nut inside the balloon.
2. Fill the balloon with air (by blowing it up with your mouth).
3. Tie the end of the balloon into a knot, trapping the hex nut inside.
4. Grip the balloon near the top (the rounded dome part) and swirl it around quickly.

WHAT'S GOING ON HERE?

Swirling the balloon causes the hex nut to slide against the inside surface in a circular pattern. This motion is known as *centrifugal force*. Friction from the six sides of the hex nut make the wall of the balloon vibrate, causing that weird screaming sound. As long as you swirl the balloon, gravity cannot pull the hex nut to the bottom. Try swirling faster and slower to see if you can change the pitch of the scream.

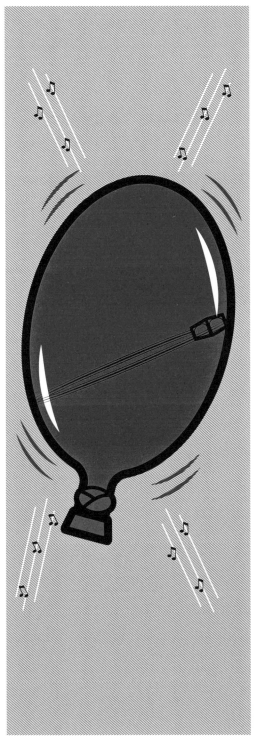

THE AMAZING GLOWING EDIBLE GOO

YOU'RE NOT SUPPOSED TO PLAY WITH YOUR FOOD,
BUT IT'S OKAY IF IT GLOWS IN THE DARK.

WHAT YOU NEED

4 large potatoes
1-liter bottle of tonic water
Boiled water
Tap water
Large pan with a handle
Large glass bowl
Small bowl
Wooden spoon
Strainer
Oven mitts
Sharp knife
Cutting board
Tall glass jar with lid
Black light
Paper towels

HOW TO DO IT

1. Wash and chop the potatoes into very small pieces.
2. Place the potatoes into the pan and, with your oven mitts on, pour the hot water over them so they're completely covered.
3. Stir for three minutes.
4. Place the strainer over the empty glass bowl in the sink and pour in the potatoes and liquid.

5. Set the potato chunks aside. (You can eat them if you don't want to throw them out.)
6. Let the liquid sit in the bowl for 10 minutes. White solids should begin to settle at the bottom.
7. Carefully pour the top layer of liquid into the sink, keeping the white solids in the bowl.
8. Add about 1/2 cup of tap water to the bowl and stir vigorously.
9. Let it sit for 15 minutes. Again, the white solids should settle to the bottom.
10. Quickly pour off the top layer of liquid and any dirt that's on top of the white goo. Let the white solids dry for 24 hours.
11. Put three heaping tablespoons of the white solids into the clean bowl.
12. Slowly stir in the tonic water, one teaspoon at a time, until it becomes too hard to stir.
13. Your goo is ready. If you move it quickly, you can shape it like dough. If you stop, it will turn into a thick liquid. Place it in the jar.
14. Turn off the lights, turn on the black light, and shine it at the potato goo. The mixture will glow in the dark.

WHAT'S GOING ON HERE?

- You made a *non-Newtonian fluid*. It's firm when a force is applied or when it's moving. It flows like a liquid when the force stops.
- Adding boiling water to the potatoes releases the starch. When you cut the potatoes into tiny chunks, you were creating as much surface area as possible, making it easier for the water to reach all the starch. That's what settles at the bottom of the bowl when you strain the potatoes. Letting the liquid sit overnight causes the water to evaporate. The starch dries into a powder.
- Tonic water contains quinine. The molecules in quinine reflect wavelengths from the black light. The light is reflected back toward your eye as a glowing visible light.

ONE CORNY EXPERIMENT

THINK OUR JOKES ARE CORNY?
THEN YOU OUGHT TO TRY THIS ONE ON FOR SIZE.

WHAT YOU NEED

1 cup cornstarch
1/2 cup water
Food coloring (optional)
Spoon
Bowl

HOW TO DO IT

1 Pour the water into the bowl. Drop in a little bit of food coloring and let it spread throughout the water.

2. Slowly mix in the cornstarch. Mix thoroughly with the spoon, and then get in there with your hands. (If it feels too watery, add more cornstarch. If it's too lumpy and won't yield, add in a little more water.)

3. Slowly push your finger into the mixture. Lift some out with your hands. What happens?

4. Stir it quickly with the spoon.

5. Now hit the mixture quickly with your fingers. Pick it up and roll it into a ball. Did something change?

WHAT'S GOING ON HERE?

The mixture is an example of a
non-Newtonian fluid. Not only does
this mean that it's not a Fig Newton,
it means it's a liquid that acts like
a liquid when gently poured, but
behaves like a solid when exposed
to sudden force. When the fluid is
moved slowly, water has time to get
between the molecules, allowing
the fluid to slide. But when a
sudden force is applied, there's no
time for the water to slip between
the molecules, making the fluid
seem hard, like a solid.

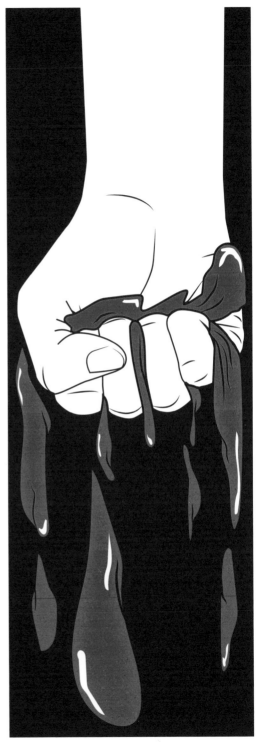

TOOTHPASTE FOR ELEPHANTS

HAS IT BEEN AGES SINCE YOUR ELEPHANT BRUSHED HIS TEETH?
TIME TO BUY SOME ELEPHANT TOOTHPASTE. ON THE OFF CHANCE
THAT YOUR NEIGHBORHOOD STORE DOESN'T CARRY ELEPHANT
TOOTHPASTE, HERE'S A RECIPE.

WHAT YOU NEED

Empty plastic soda bottle
1/4-ounce packet of active dry yeast
Warm water
Liquid soap
Food coloring
Cup
Safety glasses
Paper
1/2 cup of 6% hydrogen peroxide

HOW TO DO IT

1. Put 2–3 tablespoons of warm tap water into the cup. Stir in the yeast until it dissolves.
2. Pour the hydrogen peroxide in the empty bottle, and then add a few drops of food coloring.
3. Add a tablespoon of liquid soap into the bottle. Gently rotate the bottle so the ingredients will mix, and then place the bottle in the sink.
4. Roll the paper into a funnel and place in the top of the bottle. Using the funnel, pour the yeast/water mixture into the bottle.
5. Stand back!

WHAT'S GOING ON HERE?

Because it foams up like toothpaste and contains some of the same ingredients as toothpaste—and because it produces mass quantities suitable for a giant—scientists call this "elephant toothpaste." The warm tap water activates the yeast to action, and then the yeast releases the oxygen in the hydrogen peroxide. The oxygen becomes trapped in the soapy mixture in the form of bubbles. You'll probably also notice that the bottle feels warm. That's because those chemical reactions release energy in the form of heat. That's known as an *exothermic reaction.*

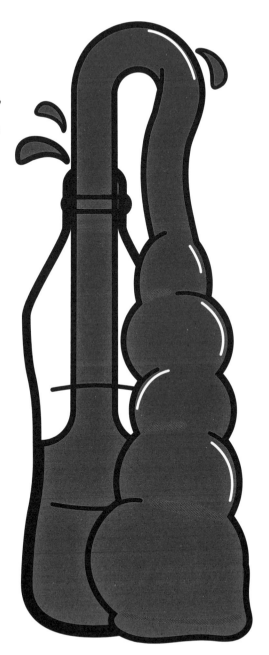

JUST US GEYSERS

THERE'S NO NEED TO RIDE HALFWAY ACROSS THE COUNTRY IN THE BACK OF THE MINIVAN WITH YOUR PARENTS TO SEE OLD FAITHFUL. YOU CAN MAKE YOUR OWN GEYSER IN THE BATHROOM.

WHAT YOU NEED

2-liter bottle of chilled soda
Roll of Mentos
Piece of thin, flexible cardboard
Bathtub or large sink
Tape

HOW TO DO IT

1. Place the bottle in the bathtub with the lid unscrewed and removed.
2. Roll the cardboard lengthwise until it's the shape of a cone. Make sure that the small hole at the bottom is large enough for a mint to drop through. Tape it to retain the funnel shape.
3. Place the funnel into the top of the bottle, with the small opening sitting inside the bottle.
4. Pour half the roll of Mentos into the funnel…and into the bubbling soda.
5. Stand back!

WHAT'S GOING ON HERE?

The bubbles in the soda are made from a gas called *carbon dioxide*. The gas is dissolved into the liquid under pressure. The surface of a Mentos contains microscopic pits and dimples, which allow bubbles to take shape, releasing that gas. The weight of the candy dropping to the bottom breaks the surface tension of the soda, and it also displaces the liquid. Of course, this all happens very fast, and all at once!

THE GOOD KIND OF BATHROOM EXPLOSION

NOW YOU HAVE SOMETHING TO BLAME BESIDES SCHOOL CAFETERIA CHILI FOR ALL THOSE WEIRD NOISES COMING OUT OF THE BATHROOM!

WHAT YOU NEED

Resealable plastic sandwich bag
Paper towel
1-1/2 tablespoons baking soda
1/4 cup vinegar
Sink

HOW TO DO IT

1. Place the baking soda in the center of the paper towel.
2. Fold the paper towel in thirds so the baking soda is in the middle and the ends overlap.
3. Fold over ends of the paper towel so you've kind of made an envelope, with the baking soda inside.
4. Pour the vinegar into the plastic bag. Now, place the paper towel inside the bag.
5. Quickly seal the bag, place it in the sink, and stand back!

WHAT'S GOING ON HERE?

Baking soda, or *sodium bicarbonate*, is a *base*, or nonacidic substance. Vinegar is an *acid*. When the two are mixed, carbon dioxide gas forms. The gas rises and inflates the bag. When the gas runs out of space, the pressure increases until the bag bursts.

YOU'LL LAVA THIS LAMP

THIS DOESN'T USE REAL LAVA. THAT WOULD BURN YOU. BUT EVEN FAKE LAVA STILL MAKES FOR A COOL LAMP.

WHAT YOU NEED

Empty 2-liter soda bottle, with cap
Water
Food coloring
Vegetable oil
1 Alka-Seltzer tablet
Small flashlight

HOW TO DO IT

1. Fill the bottle a quarter of the way with tap water.
2. Fill the remainder of the bottle with vegetable oil (or as high as you can with what oil you've got). Leave at least an inch of space at the top.
3. Add eight drops of food coloring to the bottle and let them sink to the bottom.
4. Break the tablet into small pieces. Drop the pieces into the bottle, and then cap it.
5. Shine a flashlight through the bottom of the bottle.

WHAT'S GOING ON HERE?

The tablet is made up mostly of citric acid and *sodium bicarbonate* (baking soda). When the tablet pieces drop to the bottom, they mix with the water, creating *carbon dioxide* gas. The gas rises to the top of the bottle, pushing the colored water toward the top. Because water is denser than oil, it falls back to the bottom of the bottle before rising again with the action of the bubbles.

THE SELF-INFLATING BALLOON

YOU MAY BE FULL OF HOT AIR, BUT YOU WON'T
NEED IT TO INFLATE THIS BALLOON.

WHAT YOU NEED

Empty 2-liter soda bottle
Balloon
1 tablespoon baking soda
1/4 cup vinegar
Sheet of paper

HOW TO DO IT

1. Pour the vinegar into the bottle.
2. Roll the paper into a funnel.
3. Put the small end of the funnel into the balloon.
4. Pour the baking soda through the funnel, into the balloon.
5. Stretch the neck of the balloon over the opening of the bottle.
6. Lift the top of the balloon up and shake the baking soda into the bottle.

WHAT'S GOING ON HERE?

When baking soda (sodium bicarbonate) is mixed with vinegar, it releases carbon dioxide gas. As the gas rises, the air pressure inside the bottle increases. Once the bottle is full, the pressure of the air pushes against the surface and inflates the balloon.

MILK AS PLASTIC AS THE JUG IT CAME IN

LOVE MILK? PROBABLY NOT SO MUCH AFTER THIS EXPERIMENT.

WHAT YOU NEED

Microwave
1 cup milk
1 tablespoon white vinegar
2 glass bowls
Strainer
Oven mitts
Plastic spoon
Paper towels
Mug

HOW TO DO IT

1. Pour the milk into the mug and microwave for 30 seconds. (Remove it using oven mitts.)
2. Pour the milk into a glass bowl and add the white vinegar. Stir vigorously until solids begin to appear.
3. Keep stirring for another minute.
4. Pour the mixture through a strainer situated over another glass bowl, so that the liquid is collected.

5. Place a paper towel on the counter and dump the milk solids onto it. Blot and press the paper towel against the goop to remove more moisture and help it dry.

6. You've now got a plasticlike, moldable substance. Make a shape and then put it aside to dry for one to two days. What happens?

WHAT'S GOING ON HERE?

When you add white vinegar to milk, a chemical reaction occurs. The solids you see are the proteins in the milk called *casein*. Casein molecules bond together to form a polymer that can be molded into shapes. When the casein dries, it becomes very hard, like plastic. In the early 1900s, before the use of modern-day plastics, people used milk casein to create buttons, buckles, beads, and other durable items.

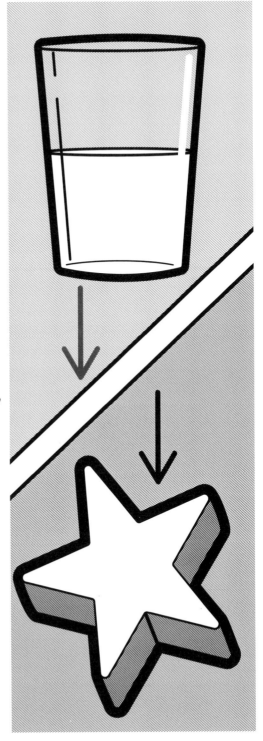

A BERRY GOOD WAY TO EXTRACT DNA

NO, YOU DON'T NEED TO USE YOUR OWN BLOOD.
STRAWBERRIES ARE JUST AS RED, BUT A LOT LESS PAINFUL.

WHAT YOU NEED

Water

1/2 teaspoon salt

1 tablespoon clear liquid soap

Bottle of rubbing alcohol, chilled

3 strawberries, chilled

Resealable plastic sandwich bag

Test tube

Coffee filter

4 clear water glasses

Rubber band

Chopsticks

Bowl

HOW TO DO IT

1. Pour the salt into a bowl and fill it up with water.
2. Add the liquid soap. Stir and set aside.
3. Place the strawberries in the plastic bag. Squeeze out as much air as possible, and then seal the bag.
4. Using your fingers, squish the strawberries inside the bag for about a minute.

5. Drape the coffee filter over a glass. Let it hang down enough to form a bowl—it should not touch the bottom of the glass. Secure the filter to the glass with the rubber band.
6. Pour the mashed strawberries on top of the coffee filter. Let it sit until all the liquid has dripped out, about 10 minutes.
7. Remove the coffee filter and strawberry pulp and set aside.
8. Tilt the glass. Slowly pour in cold rubbing alcohol down the inside of the glass until there is an inch of alcohol on top of the strawberry juice. Do not mix them.
9. Dip the chopstick into the mix. What clings to it when you pull it out again?

WHAT'S GOING ON HERE?

The white strands that form are DNA, or *deoxyribonucleic acid*. DNA contains the building blocks of life. Adding liquid soap makes the cells of the strawberries open. It dissolves any fatty substances in the cell membranes. This allows the DNA to be released. DNA is usually too small to see, but adding salt makes it visible by breaking the protein bonds and helping strands clump together.

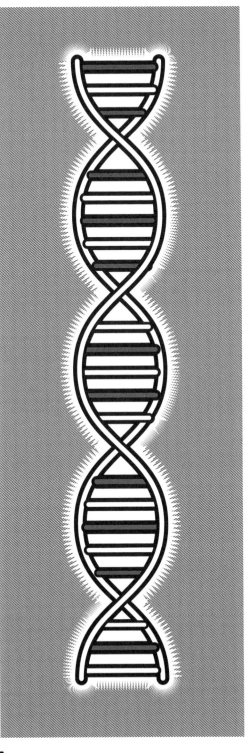

A BATHROOM STINK BOMB

NO, NOT THAT KIND OF BATHROOM STINK BOMB.

WHAT YOU NEED

Bottle of Drano crystals
Empty glass jar with lid
Warm tap water
6 eggs
Spoon
Rubber gloves

HOW TO DO IT

1. Separate the egg whites from the yolks. Discard the yolks and retain the whites in a cup.
2. Put on rubber gloves and pour 1/2 inch of Drano into the jar.
3. Add water to the jar until the liquid level is about an inch.
4. Add the egg whites and stir.
5. Screw the top on the jar.
6. Let the mixture sit in a warm place for five days.
7. Open the jar, being careful not to spill any on yourself.

WHAT'S GOING ON HERE?

Drano is made from *sodium hydroxide*, a nasty substance that rots the egg whites. (That's why Drano can unclog drains—it aggressively eliminates whatever is in its way by eating right through it.) The result: a horrible smell. Don't say we didn't warn you.

ELECTRIC BOOGALOO

WATER + ELECTRICITY = TROUBLE. BUT HERE'S A SAFE
WAY TO COMBINE THE TWO AND NOT GET ELECTROCUTED.

WHAT YOU NEED

Plastic comb
Water
Your dry hair

HOW TO DO IT

1. Turn on the water faucet so the water flows in a very thin stream.
2. Drag the comb through your hair five or six times.
3. Place the teeth of the comb about 4 inches below the faucet, but not in the water quite yet.
4. Move the comb until the teeth are about an inch from the stream of water. What happens?
5. Slowly move the comb closer to and farther from the water. Does that change the result?

WHAT'S GOING ON HERE?

Static electricity occurs when dry objects rub together, causing electrons to transfer from one object to another. The object that loses electrons carries a positive charge. The object that gains electrons becomes negatively charged. Charged objects can attract items with the opposite charge, similar to the way that opposite poles of a magnet work. In this case, hair and plastic combs are good at transferring electrons. The nylon comb has an opposite charge to the molecules in the water, so the water is attracted when the comb is near. If the nylon comb gets wet, the process won't work. The water on the comb forms a barrier that prevents the electrons from being transferred.

SPARKS WILL FLY

WANT TO MAKE SPARKS BY SMASHING THINGS? OF COURSE YOU DO.

WHAT YOU NEED

Wintergreen candy
   (such as Life Savers)
Pliers
Hammer
Cutting board
Metal baking pan
Smartphone

HOW TO DO IT

1. Place a baking pan on top of the cutting board. (This will protect your countertop.)
2. Place one wintergreen candy in the baking pan.
3. Turn out the lights so the room is as dark as possible.
4. Hit "record" on the smartphone (or another video recording device).
5. Have an adult carefully smash the candy with a hammer. What do you see?

6. Rewind and play back the video. Did something record? How is it different from what you observed with the naked eye?
7. Repeat with another piece of candy and a pair of pliers.

WHAT'S GOING ON HERE?

The effect you see is called *triboluminescence*, which means "rubbing light." This happens when energy in the form of light is produced from the friction of two objects; in this case, the hammer or pliers and the candy. The "lightning" strike results when electrons released from the sugar excite the nitrogen molecules present in the air. Positive and negative charges separate, and that energy release emits a blue light.

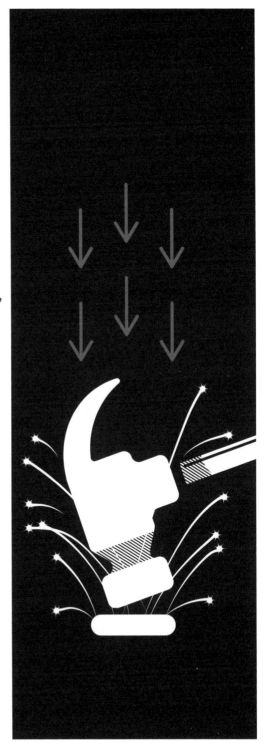

ZERO-G H2O

IF YOU'VE EVER WANTED TO DEFY GRAVITY, THEN HERE'S YOUR CHANCE.

WHAT YOU NEED

2 identical glass jars with
  wide mouths
Hot water
Cold water
Stiff piece of cardboard
  that's wider than the jars
Yellow and blue food coloring
Sink

HOW TO DO IT

1. Fill one jar with very warm tap water, and fill the other with cold water.
2. Add yellow food coloring to the hot water. Add blue food coloring to the cold water.
3. Place the cold jar into the sink, mouth side up.
4. Cover the hot jar tightly with cardboard, holding it in place so no air can enter.

5. While standing over a sink or tub, turn the hot jar upside down over the cold jar.
6. Carefully balance the yellow jar on top of the blue jar while keeping the cardboard in place. Make sure the jars line up perfectly.
7. Hold the jars while carefully removing the cardboard from between them.

WHAT'S GOING ON HERE?

Hot water is less dense than cold water. That's because hot water molecules move faster than cold water molecules, which are packed more tightly together. This makes hot water "float" on top of cold water. If you reversed the experiment, the colors would mix. That's because the cold water would be on top and, because it's denser, it would sink into the jar below.

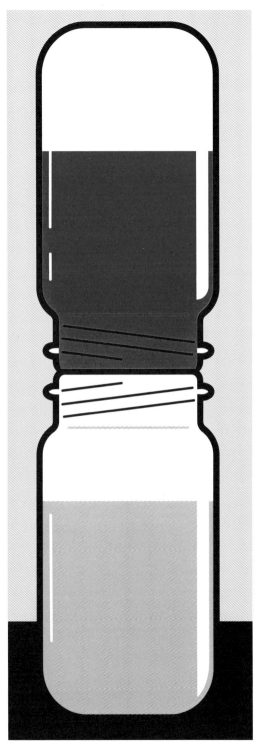

CARE FOR AN EGG FLOAT?

COME ON, DON'T BE SO DENSE.

WHAT YOU NEED

2 tall water glasses
Raw egg
2 tablespoons salt
Warm water
Food coloring

HOW TO DO IT

1. Fill a glass halfway with water.
2. Gently slide an egg into the glass. Does it float?
3. Remove the egg.
4. Dissolve two tablespoons of salt into the water. Put the egg back into the glass. What happens now?
5. Fill the second glass halfway with warm tap water. Stir in two drops of food coloring.
6. Very slowly pour the colored water into the first glass. What happens?

WHAT'S GOING ON HERE?

When you place the egg in the water, it drops to the bottom because it has more density. To get the egg to float, we have to adjust the water so it has more density than the egg. To do this, we add *sodium chloride* (salt) to the water. The water acts as a solvent and dissolves the salt. The resulting mixture is called a *saline solution*. The more salt you add, the more dense the solution. Eventually the egg will float.

When you pour plain water on top of the saline solution, it floats, too. But remember, plain water is less dense than the egg. That's why the egg remains in the middle with the saline solution on the bottom and the colored plain water on top.

FORK PHYSICS

YOUR FRIENDS WILL THINK YOU'RE SOME KIND OF MAD MAGICIAN, WHEN YOU'RE REALLY JUST A MAD SCIENTIST.

WHAT YOU NEED

Cork
2 identical forks
Wooden matchstick
Water glass
Water

HOW TO DO IT

1. Fill the glass half full with water.
2. Stick a fork in one end of the cork. Stick a fork in the opposite end of the cork so that the forks are straight across from each and form as even a line as possible.
3. Stick a match into the center of the cork so that it's *perpendicular* to the forks. (That means it sticks out at a 90-degree angle from the fork/cork combination.)
4. Carefully balance the middle of the match on the edge of the glass. What happens?
5. Light the head of the match and let it burn until it stops on its own. (It should stop when it reaches the edge of the glass). Did anything change?

WHAT'S GOING ON HERE?

This is a center of gravity experiment. The forks are identical so their mass (essentially their weight) is the same. The center of mass is the point where all the mass is concentrated. When the mass is supported at the center of mass and there is no other force acting on it, it will remain in *equilibrium*, or balance. The center of gravity is actually somewhere between the glass and the cork, but below the match. So even though the match is very light and the forks are heavier, the principles of physics ensure it stays balanced. When you burn the match, the amount of change in mass is minimal, so the forks remain balanced.

DEFYING GRAVITY

"WHAT GOES UP MUST COME DOWN." OH, YEAH? PROVE IT!

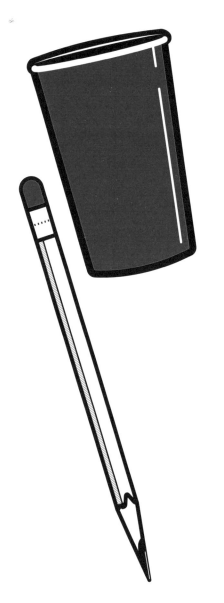

WHAT YOU NEED

Paper cup
Water
Bathtub
Pencil

HOW TO DO IT

1. Use the pencil to poke a hole in the side of the cup, near the bottom.
2. Completely cover the hole with your index finger or thumb.
3. While standing over the tub, fill the cup with water.
4. Remove your finger from the hole. Watch how fast the water flows out.
5. Put your finger back over the hole and refill the cup. Hold it up so you can see the bottom of the cup.
6. Remove your finger and let the cup drop. Carefully watch what happens, because it will happen quick!

WHAT'S GOING ON HERE?

Earth's gravity acts on everything. When you put your finger over the hole, the upward force is greater than the force pulling the water down. When you remove your finger but continue holding the cup, the water flows out of the hole because it can move, but the cup cannot. When you try the experiment again, the water doesn't flow out of the hole because the water and the cup are falling at the same rate.

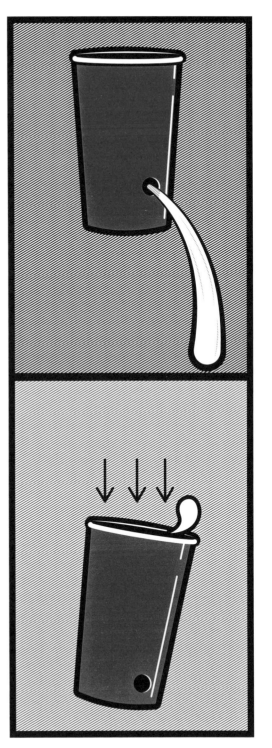

WATER, WATER... NOWHERE

EVER WONDER HOW MAGICIANS CAN POUR WATER INTO A HAT THEN PUT IT ON WITHOUT GETTING WET? THEY'RE JUST USING THIS SCIENTIFIC SHORTCUT.

WHAT YOU NEED

Glass
Disposable diaper (Huggies, or brand with an absorbent crystal lining)
1 tablespoon salt
1 cup water
Scissors
Small bowl
Safety goggles
Measuring spoons

HOW TO DO IT

1. Use the scissors to open the diaper in the center. Carefully remove the absorbent particles and place them in the bowl.
2. Scoop 1/8 teaspoon of the particles into the glass. Slowly pour water into the glass and stir. What happens?
3. Slowly add more water. How much water can you add before the mixture becomes solid?
4. Slowly stir in salt, 1/2 teaspoon at a time. When does it turn back into a liquid?

WHAT'S GOING ON HERE?

The thing that makes disposable diapers so absorbent is a material called *sodium polyacrylate*, which can absorb up to 300 times its own weight in liquid. It can hold even more than that if the water is purified and has no minerals in it. (It can only hold about 30 times its weight in urine. That's a gross fact you probably didn't want to know.) But when you add salt, the process reverses. That's because the salt draws the water out. (When you finish this experiment, *do not* dump the diaper particles in the sink. It can clog the drain. Discard in the trash when complete.)

DO NOT MIX!

IT'S COMMON KNOWLEDGE THAT OIL AND WATER DON'T MIX.
EXCEPT WHEN THEY DO.

WHAT YOU NEED

Empty 2-liter soda bottle, with cap
1/4 cup water
Food coloring
1/4 cup vegetable oil
Liquid soap

HOW TO DO IT

1. Pour the water into the bottle, add a few drops of food coloring, and shake well to mix.
2. Add the oil to the bottle.
3. Screw on the cap, and shake the bottle to mix the two liquids.
4. Set down the bottle and watch what happens as the solution settles. (What should happen? The liquids will separate.)
5. Open up the bottle and add a few drops of liquid soap.
6. Replace the cap and shake.

WHAT'S GOING ON HERE?

Water and oil don't mix (usually) because water molecules attract other molecules, while oil molecules attract only other oil molecules. Their molecular structures don't allow oil and water to bind. Oil is less dense than water, so it floats on top when they separate. However, liquid soap molecules are attracted to both water *and* oil. One end of the molecule attracts water, and the other end attracts oil. The soap molecules bind to both, making it easy to mix the two. This is why soap is effective at cleaning oil from clothes, dishes, and you.

A DARK MESSAGE

WHO WROTE THAT MESSAGE? YOU...OR A GHOST?
(ANSWER: YOU DID.)

WHAT YOU NEED

Petroleum jelly
Paper
Black light

HOW TO DO IT

1. Put petroleum jelly on your finger.
2. Use that finger to draw a small picture or write a word on the paper.
3. Close the bathroom door and turn off all the lights.
4. Turn on the black light, let it warm up for a minute, and then aim it at the paper. What happens?
5. Try smearing some petroleum jelly all over one of your hands. Aim the light at it. What do you see?

WHAT'S GOING ON HERE?

Most lights emit a frequency that your eye interprets as visible light in the form of any number of colors. Black lights, however, emit an *ultraviolet wave* that your eye can't see. The petroleum jelly contains *phosphors*, which absorb this light radiation and emit it back at your eyes in a different frequency. This visible light makes the jelly glow in black light.

THE GLOWING, FLOWING FOUNTAIN

IT'S POSSIBLE WITH CANDY, SODA, AND A BLACK LIGHT.

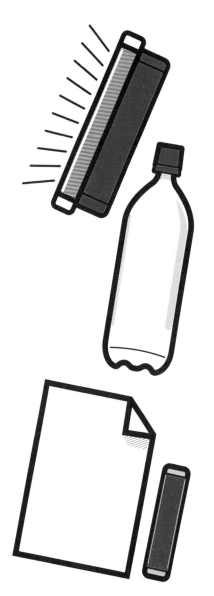

WHAT YOU NEED

1-liter bottle of tonic water
    at room temperature
Roll of Mentos
Black light
Sheet of paper

HOW TO DO IT

1. Remove the paper label from a bottle of tonic water.
2. Open the bottle and pour a small amount into the sink.
3. Set the bottle in the bathtub.
4. Turn on the black light.
5. Take the wrapper off the Mentos.
6. Roll the plain paper into a funnel that fits inside the mouth of the bottle.

7. Turn off the bathroom light.
8. Drop all the Mentos into the funnel, and then quickly remove the paper.
9. Stand back, but keep shining the black light at the bottle.

WHAT'S GOING ON HERE?

Tonic water contains *quinine*, which carries atoms that absorb energy when exposed to ultraviolet light. The energy is reflected back to you as visible light…that glows. The bubbles in the soda are carbon dioxide gas, introduced to the tonic water under pressure. When the bottle is opened, the bubbles begin to escape. Tiny dimples on the Mentos help more bubbles to form quickly. The chemical reaction results in an explosive fountain.

GLOW YOUR OWN WAY

NOW YOU DON'T HAVE TO WAIT FOR A NUCLEAR ACCIDENT TO MAKE YOUR WATER GLOW!

WHAT YOU NEED

2 tall water glasses
2 neon-colored highlighters
Pliers
Tweezers
Black light
Water

HOW TO DO IT

1. Fill the glasses two-thirds full with water.
2. Use pliers to pull off the bottoms of the highlighters. With tweezers, carefully remove the ink cartridges.
3. Sit each ink tube inside a glass of water. Let sit for 30 minutes.
4. With the tweezers, remove the ink cartridges.
5. Turn on the black light.
6. Turn off the bathroom light so the bathroom is dark, except for the black light.

WHAT'S GOING ON HERE?

The neon highlighters are *fluorescent*, which means they'll glow under a black light. Highlighters contain a special dye that contains chemicals that help the dye absorb energy from the ultraviolet spectrum of light. This excites the electrons in the dye, which gives off energy in the form of visible light. The light is hard to see in the day, but easy to see when it's dark. Exposing the dye to the ultraviolet (UV) rays in a black light allows it to absorb more energy and therefore give off a brighter light.

A TIME TO REFRACT

THIS TRICK WILL BEND LIGHT AS WELL AS YOUR MIND.

WHAT YOU NEED

Glass jar
Newspaper
Water
Paper
Black marker

HOW TO DO IT

1. Fill the jar halfway with tap water.
2. Place the newspaper behind the jar. Look through the water from the other side of the jar.
3. Slowly pull the newspaper backward. What happened to the print?
4. On a piece of paper, draw two arrows pointing in the same direction. Draw them about two inches apart.
5. Place the paper so that one arrow is seen above the water line, and one is seen below. Look at the image again. Move it forward or backward until something changes. What happens?

6. On another piece of paper, draw a thick arrow about 1 inch wide and 3 inches long. Place the paper behind the jar so that half the arrow is above the water line and half is below. What happens?
7. Now fill the jar all the way with water. Observe the drawing.

WHAT'S GOING ON HERE?

Refraction is the process in which light bends as it passes through a material. When you placed the paper behind the glass, light traveled through multiple layers. First it traveled through the air, then the front surface of the jar, through the water, the back of the jar, the air, and then it bounced back through those layers to your eye. The water in the jar acts like a giant magnifying glass. Did you notice that the print of the newspaper looked larger when viewed through the jar, compared to the print that appeared above the water line? When the light traveled through the water, the light moving toward the paper was moving in the opposite direction than the light coming back to your eye. Light rays that were on the right now come back on the opposite side, making the print look like it changed direction, too.

NOW YOU SEE IT, NOW YOU DON'T

IS IT MAGIC...OR IS IT AN OPTICAL ILLUSION?

WHAT YOU NEED

6 ounces glycerin

Water

2 empty 2-ounce condiment bottles (such as Tabasco sauce) with the labels removed

2 glasses

Funnel

HOW TO DO IT

1. Using the funnel, fill one bottle with water, and the other with glycerin.
2. Fill one water glass halfway with water. Fill the other glass halfway with glycerin.
3. Place the bottle of water into the glass of water.
4. Put the bottle of glycerin into the glass of glycerin.
5. Look through the glasses. What differences do you see?

WHAT'S GOING ON HERE?

In another experiment (see page 68) we learned about how light travels through transparent materials, hits a surface, and travels back to our eyes. In this case, the water, the glass, and glycerin have different densities. When you put a bottle of water into a glass of water, the light travels through the glass at a different speed and angle than it does the water. It bends at each intersection as it returns to our eyes. This allows us to see the edges of the inner bottle and the water between them. When you put a bottle of glycerin into a glass of glycerin, the bottle seems to disappear. That's because light travels through glycerin at the same speed and angle as the glass containers. The result is that the part of the bottle in the liquid seems to disappear before your eyes.

LOST IN THE BATHROOM

THERE'S MORE THAN ONE WAY TO FIND YOUR WAY OUT OF THE BATHROOM.

WHAT YOU NEED
Sink stopper
Round cork
Sewing needle
Magnet
Water

HOW TO DO IT
1. Place the stopper in the drain and fill up the sink halfway.
2. Place the cork in the water. It should float.
3. Rub the magnet over the needle 40 times, but always in the same direction. (Left to right, for example.)
4. Set the needle on top of the cork. Which way does the needle point?
5. What happens if you turn the cork 180 degrees? Does it turn back?

WHAT'S GOING ON HERE?

Normally needles are not magnetic. But if you rub a magnet over a needle, it causes the magnet material in the metal to line up in the same direction. That makes it magnetic for a short amount of time. When you place the needle on the cork, there is no force preventing the cork from moving. The cork floats freely in the water, so it rotates with the needle until the needle is pointing toward the Earth's north and south magnetic poles.

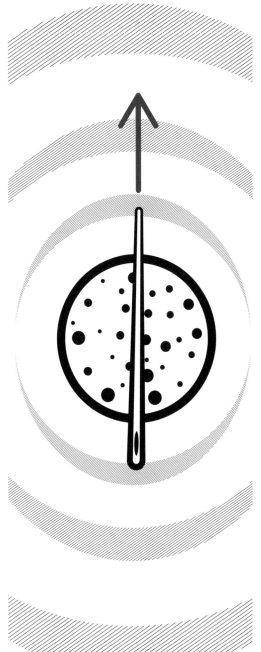

THE PENNY SAVER

PENNIES ARE WORTH MORE IF THEY'RE CLEAN. OKAY, NOT REALLY, BUT CLEAN ONES SURE ARE SHINY!

WHAT YOU NEED

Old, dull pennies
1/2 cup white vinegar
2 teaspoons salt
2 glass bowls
Water

HOW TO DO IT

1. Pour white vinegar into one bowl. Stir in the salt.
2. Drop a penny and leave it in there for 10 seconds.
3. Fill up another bowl with water.
4. Take out the penny from the vinegar and rinse it in the water.

WHAT'S GOING ON HERE?

Over time, pennies lose their shine because of *oxidation*. Oxidation happens when the copper molecules in the penny are exposed to oxygen in the air. The vinegar is a weak acid. It removes the layer of *copper oxide* from the penny to restore its shine. If you did not rinse the penny, the vinegar would eventually turn your penny green.

NOW WATCH THIS CLIP

YOU CAN OVERFLOW A CUP OF WATER WITHOUT MAKING IT SPILL. (THIS DOES NOT, HOWEVER, WORK ON TOILETS.)

WHAT YOU NEED

Water glass
10–20 paper clips
Water
Eyedropper

HOW TO DO IT

1. Fill the glass to the brim with water.
2. Fill the eyedropper. Add more water to the glass a drop at a time until the glass is *completely* full.
3. Slowly drop a paper clip into the water. Does the water overflow?
4. Very carefully, observe the top of the water. Does it form a dome?
5. Add more paper clips, one at a time. Observe the way the top of the water looks.
6 Keep going until the water overflows.

WHAT'S GOING ON HERE?

When you drop paper clips into the glass, it displaces the water, pushing it higher. If you're careful, once the water reaches the rim, it will push up in the center while the edges are pulled by gravity and cling to the cup. It will collapse once there are enough paper clips in the water, when the surface tension holding the dome can no longer withstand the weight of the water above the cup. Then the dome will break and the water will overflow down the sides of the glass.

MAKING CENTS

COME SEE THE FABULOUS WATER DOME!

WHAT YOU NEED

Penny or dime
Eyedropper
Magnifying glass

HOW TO DO IT

1. Fill the eyedropper with water.
2. Drip water onto the coin one drop at a time.
3. Observe with a magnifying glass. What happens after a few drops?
4. How many drops can you put on the coin before the water dome collapses? Does the number of drops needed change if you flip the coin over and start again?

WHAT'S GOING ON HERE?

Like in the previous experiment, the dome is held together by surface tension. The water molecules have positive and negative poles that attract each other. The water clings to the edges of the coin. As more water is added, the middle rises to form a dome that holds the water inside. The dome will collapse when the weight of the water and gravity is greater than the strength of the surface tension.

MONEY TALKS

A QUARTER MAY NOT BUY MUCH THESE DAYS, BUT HERE'S A SNEAKY WAY TO MAKE YOUR MONEY WORK FOR YOU.

WHAT YOU NEED

Empty 2-liter soda bottle
Quarter
Cup
Water
Freezer

HOW TO DO IT

1. Place the empty soda bottle in the freezer for 10 minutes.
2. Place the quarter in a cup of water.
3. Take the soda bottle out of the freezer and remove the cap.
4. Remove the quarter from the water. Quickly place the quarter over the mouth of the bottle so the hole is completely covered. What happens?

WHAT'S GOING ON HERE?

When air cools, the molecules slow down and move closer together. When the bottle is removed from the freezer, the air inside begins to warm up. As it does, the molecules begin moving faster and spread out. When you cover the mouth of the bottle with the quarter, it traps the air inside. After a while, the pressure builds as the molecules spread out and push against the quarter, moving it up and making it chatter.

WHAT'S THE SOLUTION?

SOMETIMES SOLVING A PUZZLE MEANS KNOWING WHEN TO STOP.

WHAT YOU NEED

4 water glasses
Water
Sugar
Salt
Ground black pepper
Cinnamon

HOW TO DO IT

1. Fill a glass halfway with warm water and add a tablespoon of sugar. Stir 20 times. What happens?
2. Add more sugar to the solution, one tablespoon at a time. Keep track of how much you're adding. How much is added before the liquid can't hold any more?
3. Let the solution rest for 10 minutes. What happens when the solution is allowed to rest?
4. Fill the other glasses with warm water. Repeat the experiment using salt, pepper, and cinnamon in each glass.

WHAT'S GOING ON HERE?

Particles dissolved in a liquid are called *solute* while the liquid is called a *solvent*. When the liquid cannot hold any more particles, we consider the solution to be *saturated*. Since those leftover particles are denser than water, they sink to the bottom.

THE ROCKET BALLOON

YOU MAY NOT BE A NASA SCIENTIST—YET—BUT YOU
CAN STILL MAKE THINGS FLY REALLY FAST.

WHAT YOU NEED

Balloon
String
Plastic drinking straw
Tape

HOW TO DO IT

1. Pull the string through the straw.
2. Tie one end of the string to a doorknob, and the other end to a window or towel bar across the room.
3. Pull it tight so there's no slack in the line.
4. Cut two pieces of tape. Drape them over the straw so they hang over both sides.
5. Blow air into the balloon until it's full. Pinch the neck closed, but don't tie it.
6. Attach the balloon to the straw with both pieces of tape.
7. Let go!

WHAT'S GOING ON HERE?

When you blow air into a balloon, it becomes trapped. The more air you add, the higher the pressure on the walls of the balloon, which causes it to expand. The air pressure outside is lower. When you let go of the balloon, the air escapes. The force of the air rushing out pushes the balloon in the opposite direction. This energy is known as *thrust*.

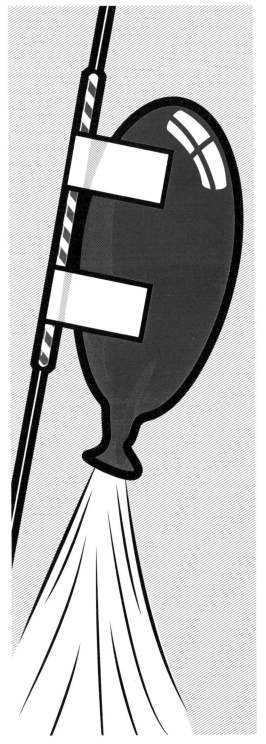

BUBBLE ATTACK!

THIS MAKES SO MANY THOUSANDS OF TINY LITTLE BUBBLES, YOU'RE PROBABLY GOING TO GET IN TROUBLE FOR SPILLING A SODA. JUST EXPLAIN THAT IT'S SOAP—WHICH TOTALLY WASHES RIGHT OUT.

WHAT YOU NEED

Empty 2-liter soda bottle

Cotton washcloth or towel

Thick rubber band

1/4 cup liquid soap

1/4 cup water

Bowl

Spoon

Scissors

HOW TO DO IT

1. Cut the bottle in half. Keep only the top half.
2. Pour 1/4 cup of water into the bowl.
3. Stir 1/4 cup of liquid soap into the bowl.
4. Fold the washcloth over the wide end of the water bottle.
5. Secure the cloth to the bottle with a rubber band.
6. Dip the cloth in the water and let it soak.

7. Pull the bottle out of the mixture and shake off the extra liquid.
8. Holding the towel, blow through the narrow end of the bottle.
9. Want to make rainbow foam? Add food colors to the washcloth before you dip it into the soap mixture.

WHAT'S GOING ON HERE?

Water molecules attract each other. When air is trapped, bubbles form. When you blow air through the washcloth you're forcing it through the openings in the fabric, creating hundreds of bubbles that stick to each other as they form.

CLOUDY WITH A CHANCE OF SCIENCE

OH BUMMER, IT'S ANOTHER SUNNY DAY OUTSIDE. DON'T YOU WISH IT WAS CLOUDY? IT CAN BE...IF YOU JUST STAY INSIDE.

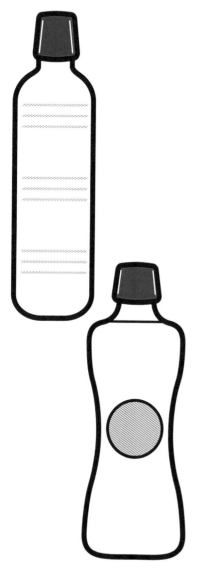

WHAT YOU NEED

Small water bottle with a cap
Rubbing alcohol

HOW TO DO IT

1. Pour rubbing alcohol into the bottle, up to about two inches from the top.
2. Screw the cap on tightly.
3. Hold the bottle horizontally.
4. Moving your hands in opposite directions, twist the bottle as far as it will go.
5. Point the top of the bottle away from anything breakable, including people.
6. Unscrew the cap until it is loose.
7. Use your thumb to flick the cap completely off.

WHAT'S GOING ON HERE?

When you twisted the bottle, that increased the pressure inside. That pushed the individual molecules closer together, and made the water vapor become denser. When the cap is removed, the air molecules have space, and can move farther apart. It also causes the vapor to cool. The molecules of the air, alcohol, and water then stick together, forming "clouds."

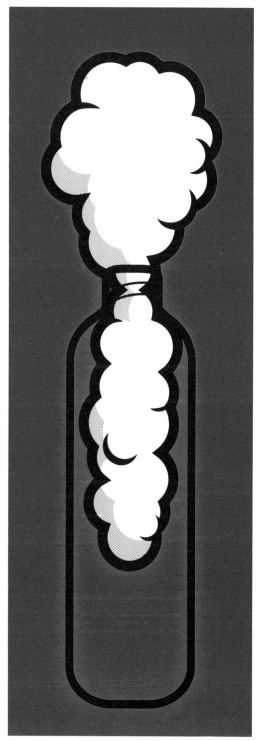

THE DOUBLE HURRICANE

YOU DON'T NEED A COMPLEX WEATHER SYSTEM TO MAKE A HURRICANE. ALL YOU NEED IS A COUPLE OF BOTTLES.

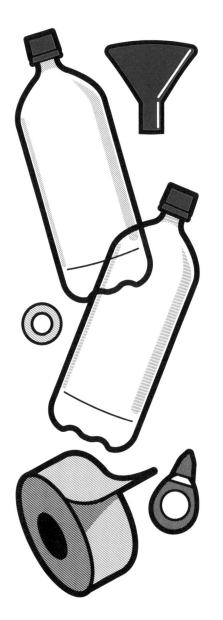

WHAT YOU NEED

2 empty 1-liter plastic bottles
Water
Blue food coloring
One 1/4-inch metal washer
Duct tape

HOW TO DO IT

1. Place the funnel into the mouth of one bottle.
2. Fill the bottle with water.
3. Add three drops of blue food coloring.
4. Remove the funnel.
5. Put the washer on the mouth of the bottle.
6. Turn the empty bottle upside down and place the mouth snugly against the top of the washer.
7. Use duct tape to securely connect the bottles together. Make sure the connections are tight so there are no leaks.

8. Carefully flip the bottles over so the liquid is now on top. How long does it take for the water to drain to the bottom?
9. After the water drains, turn the bottles over so the one with liquid is on the top.
10. Using both hands, swirl the top bottle quickly so the liquid begins to spin.
11. Set the experiment down and watch what happens.

WHAT'S GOING ON HERE?

When you first turned the bottle, the water drained slowly. This is because taping the bottles together created a vacuum. No outside air could get into the bottle. The water on top could not reach the bottom bottle unless the air in the bottom bottle was able to replace it. The rate of exchange is very slow. When you repeated the experiment something changed. When the water swirled it created a vortex. This vortex makes it easier for air to pass through to the top bottle as the swirling water moves into the bottom bottle.

FREE THE CLOUDS!

WHAT ARE CLOUDS? COMPRESSED AIR. WHAT'S IN THAT CAN OF STUFF YOU SHOOT TO CLEAN YOUR COMPUTER KEYBOARD? COMPRESSED AIR. THAT MEANS...YOU'VE GOT A BOTTLE FULL OF CLOUDS THAT ARE JUST WAITING TO GET OUT!

WHAT YOU NEED

Glass bowl

Can of compressed air
     with straw attachment

Hot water

HOW TO DO IT

1. Fill the bowl halfway with hot water.
2. Insert one end of the straw into the nozzle of the can of compressed air. Place the other end of the straw below the surface of the water in the bowl.
3. Push the trigger to blow compressed air into the water.

WHAT'S GOING ON HERE?

Water molecules are suspended in the air around you in the form of warm vapor. When vapor rises, it cools and condenses, forming clouds in the atmosphere. Water vapor that cools closer to the ground is what we call "fog." The can of compressed air contains gases under extreme pressure. That pressure turns the gases into liquids and lowers the temperature. When released from the can, the compressed air rapidly cools the warm water molecules in the glass bowl. Those water molecules condense as they rise to the surface, forming misty clouds.

(Caution: Let the condensed air can rest before moving it or trying the experiment again. It will be extremely cold and could be painful to the touch.)

A TINY RAFTING TRIP

HERE'S WHY SOME THINGS FLOAT...AND SOME JUST WON'T.

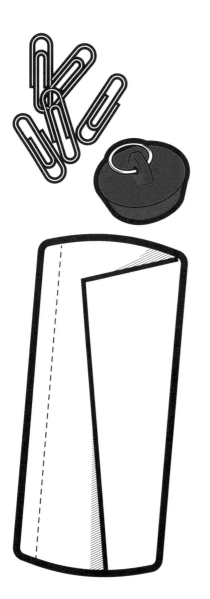

WHAT YOU NEED

Sink
Sink stopper
Cold tap water
Paper clips
Paper towels

HOW TO DO IT

1. Put the stopper in the sink.
2. Fill the sink halfway with water.
3. Try floating the paper clip on the surface of the water. Did it work?
4. Now tear off a small piece of paper towel.
5. Place the paper clip in the middle of the towel.
6. Slowly lower the towel onto the surface of the water. Be patient, and watch what happens.

WHAT'S GOING ON HERE?

The surface of the water forms a skin. We call this *surface tension*. The surface tension is strong enough to hold the paper clip for a short while. The paper towel has tiny pores. It absorbs water and gets heavier. When the towel is saturated, it will sink, but the paper clip will not. The clip will float… until you touch it. That breaks the surface tension.

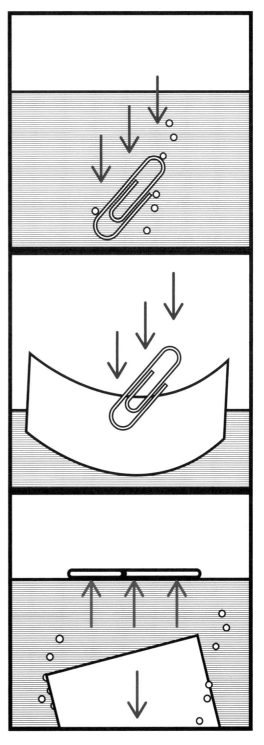

THE S.S. STRAW

IF FOR SOME REASON YOU EVER NEED TO POWER A BOAT IN YOUR BATHROOM, WELL, YOU'VE GOT ALL THE FUEL YOU NEED IN THERE.

WHAT YOU NEED

2 plastic cups
2 Styrofoam plates
Glue gun
Flexible straw
Bathtub

HOW TO DO IT

1. Fill the tub about a quarter of the way full.
2. Place glue around the top rim of one plate.
3. Turn the second plate upside down. Place it on top of the first plate, with the rims touching.
4. Carefully poke a small hole in one cup, half an inch above the bottom.
5. Glue the bottoms of the cups together. It will look like an hourglass.
6. Glue the rim of the cup without a hole to the center of the plate.
7. Put the straw in the hole and bend it so it's pointing up.

8. Put the plate in the bathtub.
9. Fill the top cup with water.
10. Point the straw down so the water flows out of the cup.

WHAT'S GOING ON HERE?

Water always seeks lower ground due to the pull of gravity. When you point the straw toward the bathtub, gravity causes the water to flow downhill. The force of the water escaping through the straw creates pressure against the water in the tub. That pushes the "boat" in the opposite direction.

THE S.S. SOAPY SUDS

HERE'S ANOTHER WAY TO POWER A BOAT, THIS TIME THROUGH THE SCIENTIFIC MAGIC OF SOAP.

WHAT YOU NEED

Empty juice or milk carton
Sink
Sink stopper
Liquid soap
Toothpick
Water

HOW TO DO IT

1. Cut a rectangle from one side of the empty carton.
2. Cut the top at an angle so the piece is shaped like a house.
3. Cut a square notch in the middle of the base of the "house" to complete your boat.
4. Put the stopper in the sink and fill the sink halfway with water.
5. Place the boat in the water on one side of the sink.
6. Dip the toothpick into the liquid soap and place it inside the notch in the boat.
7. Place your finger near the notch and set sail!

WHAT'S GOING ON HERE?

Water has a high surface tension; soap has low surface tension. Adding soap causes the water to contract, or move away from, the soap. Fluids with low surface tension move toward areas with high surface tension. This is called the *Marangoni effect*. The soap fluid moves out of the notch at the back of the boat, pushing the boat forward.

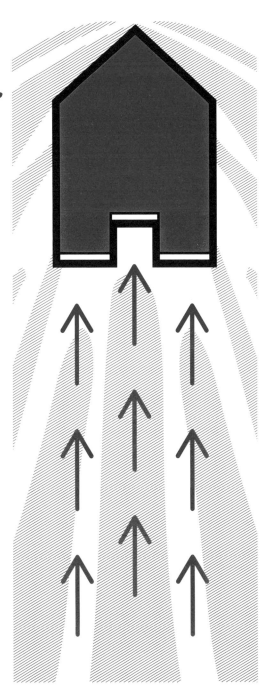

THE ESCAPING PEPPER

SOAP SOMETIMES SENDS SOME PEOPLE FLEEING AT BATH TIME. IT DOES THE SAME THING TO OTHER OBJECTS, TOO.

WHAT YOU NEED

Bowl

2 cups water

Ground black pepper

Liquid soap

HOW TO DO IT

1. Pour the water into a bowl.
2. Sprinkle pepper over the surface.
3. Cover your finger in liquid soap.
4. Gently put your finger in the middle of the water. Pull it out again. What happens to the pepper?

WHAT'S GOING ON HERE?

The surface tension on the water forms a type of skin that is strong enough to hold light items. That's why the pepper floats on top. But soap molecules are big enough to break the surface tension. The water molecules move to the side, taking the pepper flakes with them.

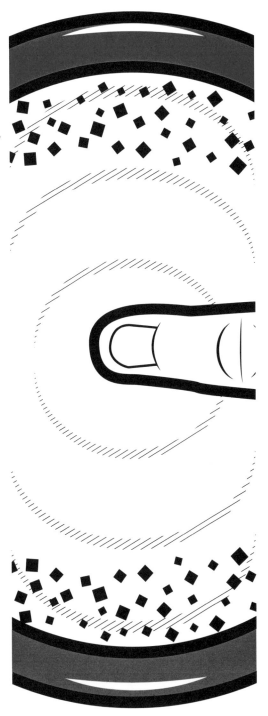

HOLD ON TO YOUR BUBBLES

THE WORST THING ABOUT BUBBLES?
THEY POP SO QUICKLY. NOT THESE BUBBLES.

WHAT YOU NEED

Clean cotton glove or mitten
1 teaspoon liquid soap
1 teaspoon corn syrup
Drinking straw
Scissors
Glass
1/2 cup of water

HOW TO DO IT

1. Add the water and corn syrup to the glass, and stir well.
2. Pour the liquid soap into the water and stir until dissolved.
3. Put on the glove. With your non-gloved hand, dip one of the straws into the liquid, and then quickly remove it.
4. Blow a bubble through the straw onto your gloved hand.
5. See if you can bounce the bubble around on the glove.

WHAT'S GOING ON HERE?

Bubbles are comprised of air surrounded by a thin film of water and soap. The liquid's molecules are attracted to each other, creating *surface tension*. When the bubble touches something dry or dirty, the surface tension breaks, causing the bubble to pop. A clean cotton glove will eliminate a lot of the things that cause the bubble to break. Adding glycerin into the soap mixture makes the bubble surface strong by slowing evaporation.

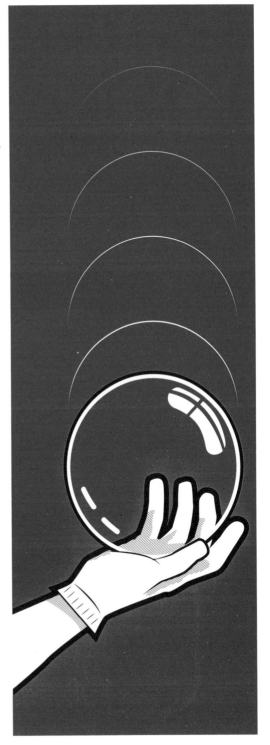

THE VACUUM PACK

AIR IS INVISIBLE, BUT IT EXERTS A LOT OF FORCE.
SO DOES A VACUUM. WHO WILL WIN?

WHAT YOU NEED

Large jar with a wide mouth
1-quart resealable plastic bag
Tape
Rubber bands

HOW TO DO IT

1. Cover the mouth of the jar with the plastic bag. Push the bag so the middle sits inside the jar.
2. Secure the bag to the jar with rubber bands. Add tape to ensure that the jar is airtight.
3. Reach in and try to pull up the bag. Can you do it?

WHAT'S GOING ON HERE?

Air exerts pressure on the plastic bag. When you attempt to pull the bag out, it creates a *vacuum*. That means the same amount of air molecules is now occupying a larger space made when the bag is lifted. It becomes less dense than the air above the bag. Nature doesn't like a vacuum, so it pulls on the bag to restore the air pressure to its original state. If you were to poke a hole in the bag, the air above and below would exchange until the air pressure was equalized.

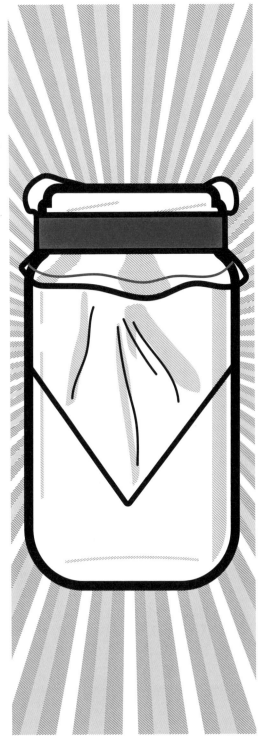

A MAJOR CRUSH

THINK YOU'RE NOT STRONG ENOUGH TO CRUSH A CAN WITH YOUR BARE HANDS? SURE YOU ARE! ALSO, WE BET YOU CAN DO IT WITHOUT EVEN USING YOUR HANDS.

WHAT YOU NEED

Empty aluminum soda can
Medium balloon
Thick rubber band
Boiling water
Oven mitts
Scissors

HOW TO DO IT

1. Have an adult boil some water.
2. Cut off the opening of the balloon—where you would blow into it—and throw it away.
3. Put the empty can in the sink.
4. Put on oven mitts to protect your hands, and then carefully pour the hot water into the can until full.
5. Stretch the top half of the balloon over the can, and use the rubber band to hold the balloon in place.

WHAT'S GOING ON HERE?

No air can get in or out—a vacuum has been created. The hot air molecules inside the can move faster than cool air outside of it. The hot air is thinner and its molecules push against the can as they move. As the hot air cools, the molecules slow down and move closer together. The air pressure outside is now greater than inside…which causes the can to collapse.

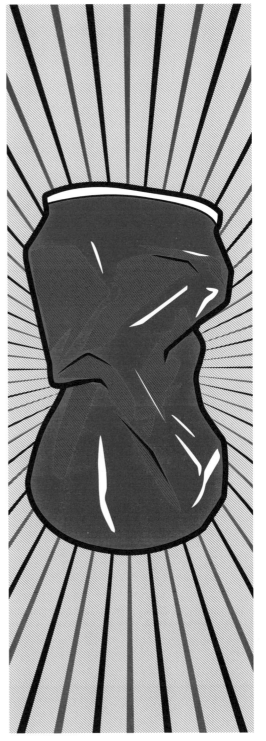

SPRING A LEAK!

NOTHING STOPS A LEAK LIKE A VACUUM.

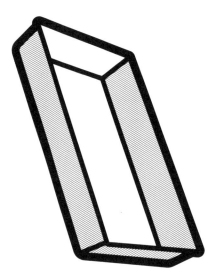

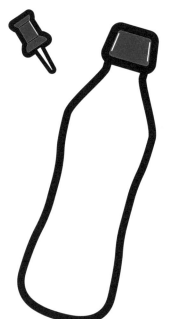

WHAT YOU NEED

Empty 20-ounce plastic soda bottle
Pushpin
Water
Sink
Baking pan

HOW TO DO IT

1. Remove the cap from the bottle.
2. Poke three holes down the side of the bottle with the pushpin. (Don't place them too high up.)
3. Fill the sink with water.
4. Push the bottle underwater until it fills completely with water.
5. Screw the cap on while the bottle is submerged.
6. Put the bottle in the pan. What happens?
7. Unscrew the top and remove it. What happens now?

WHAT'S GOING ON HERE?

When the top is on the bottle, no air can get in or out of the bottle, even with the holes. It forms a vacuum. The air pressure outside of the bottle pushes against the surface. It's enough to keep the water from leaking out. Once the cap is removed, air is able to enter the bottle. The increased pressure pushes down on the water, forcing it through the holes. As the water leaks out, more air rushes in to take its place.

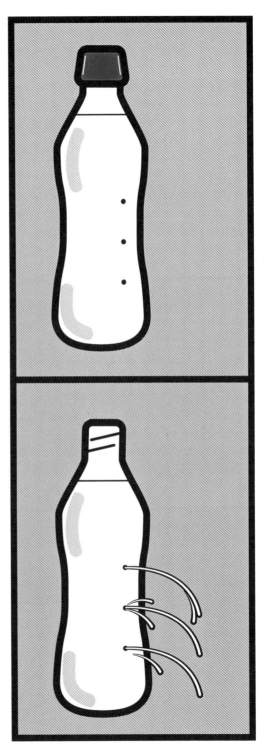

INSIDE OUT

DID YOU KNOW THAT YOU CAN TURN A BALLOON INSIDE OUT WITHOUT USING YOUR HANDS?

WHAT YOU NEED

Empty 2-liter soda bottle
Bowl
Small balloon
Water
Ice

HOW TO DO IT

1. Fill the bowl with ice and set aside.
2. Fill the plastic bottle with very warm (but not hot) tap water.
3. Let the bottle sit for one minute. Empty out the water, so the bottle remains warm.
4. Stretch a balloon over the mouth of the bottle. What happens to the balloon?
5. Now sit the bottle in the bowl of ice.

WHAT'S GOING ON HERE?

Air expands as it warms, making more space between the molecules and causing them to move faster. When the air cools, it becomes denser. The molecules move slower and more closely together. Because the balloon prevents more air from entering the bottle, a *vacuum* forms. As the bottle cools, the contraction of the air in the bottle pulls on the balloon to fill the extra space.

THE ISSUE OF TISSUES

HERE'S ONE FOR WHEN YOU'RE SO BORED
THAT IT SEEMS LIKE THE ONLY INTERESTING THING
TO PLAY WITH IS A BOX OF TISSUES.

WHAT YOU NEED

Bowl
Plastic cup
Box of tissues
Water

HOW TO DO IT

1. Fill the bowl three-quarters full with water.
2. Crumple a sheet of tissue until it forms a tight ball. Place the tissue snugly into the bottom of the cup.
3. Turn the cup upside down.
4. Push it into the bowl of water. Hold it firmly against the bottom of the bowl for a few seconds.
5. Pull the cup straight up. Is the tissue still dry?
6. Repeat steps 3 through 5. Now tilt the cup instead of pulling it out. What happens?
7. Pull the cup out of the water. Is the tissue still dry?

WHAT'S GOING ON HERE?

Although you can't see it, the space not occupied by the tissue is full of air. When you plunged the cup into the water, the air was trapped with no way to escape. No water could enter the cup and make the tissue wet. When you tried the experiment again, you tilted the cup. That was enough to give the air an escape route. When the bubble of air escaped, it allowed the water to rush in and replace it. That made the tissue wet.

THE LIQUID VACUUM

HERE'S SOME SCIENCE MAGIC TO IMPRESS YOUR FRIENDS:
MOVE WATER INTO AN UPSIDE-DOWN GLASS.

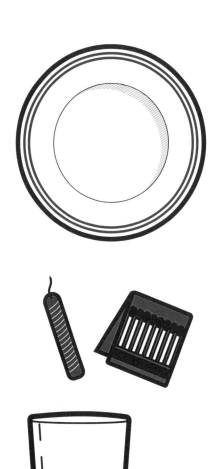

WHAT YOU NEED

Water glass
Water
Small candle
Matches
Food coloring
Ceramic dinner plate

HOW TO DO IT

1. Mix a few drops of food coloring into a glass of water.
2. Pour the water onto the plate until the bottom is covered.
3. Put the candle in the center of the liquid on the plate.
4. Light the wick.
5. Cover the candle with an empty water glass.

WHAT'S GOING ON HERE?

Fire needs fuel to burn, and the flame of the candle burns oxygen gas for fuel. When you place a glass over the candle, it uses the oxygen trapped beneath the glass. The remaining gases have a lower pressure than the air outside, so the liquid on the plate is drawn into the glass. Also, the candle heats the air, and the air expands. When the candle goes out, the air cools and becomes more dense. That creates a vacuum, drawing liquid into the glass.

THE PASTA ROCKET

YOU MAY NOT BE ABLE TO PLAY WITH NASA'S
ROCKET FUEL, BUT YOU CAN PROPEL A ROCKET WITH
SOME STUFF IN THE BATHROOM.

WHAT YOU NEED

Piece of ziti pasta

Hydrogen peroxide

Small canning jar with a two-part
  lid (a flat piece and an outer
  ring)

3/4 teaspoon yeast

Butane lighter

Hammer

Nail

Safety goggles

HOW TO DO IT

1. Take the lid off the jar and set
   aside the outer ring. You won't
   need it—it would cause too
   much pressure to build up in the
   jar.
2. Use the hammer and nail to
   carefully punch a small hole into
   the center of the flat lid.
3. Fill the jar 3/4 full with hydrogen
   peroxide. Add the yeast.

4. Secure the flat lid on top of the jar. The mixture will begin to bubble, and gas will be released through the hole.
5. Stand a piece of ziti on top of the hole.
6. Activate the lighter and place near the top of the pasta to ignite the gas. Flame on!

WHAT'S GOING ON HERE?

Hydrogen peroxide consists of two molecules of hydrogen bonded to two molecules of oxygen. Mixing the enzymes in yeast with hydrogen peroxide causes a chemical reaction that releases the oxygen molecules in the form of pure—and highly flammable—oxygen gas. As pressure builds, the gas is forced out of the hole in the lid. The pasta provides a tunnel for the oxygen to flow straight up. The flame from the lighter will ignite the gas as it escapes the pasta. It looks similar to the flames from a rocket.

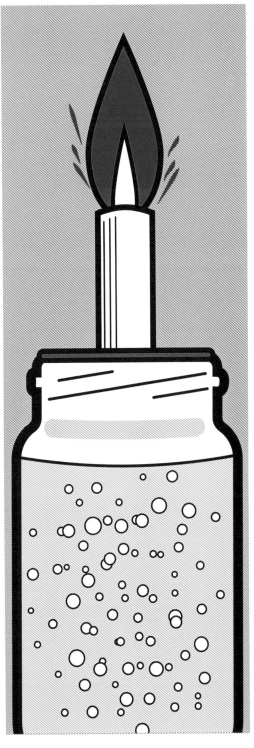

THE DISAPPEARING WAX

WITH THIS EXPERIMENT, YOU MAY JUST THINK YOU CAN DEFY THE LAWS OF SCIENCE.

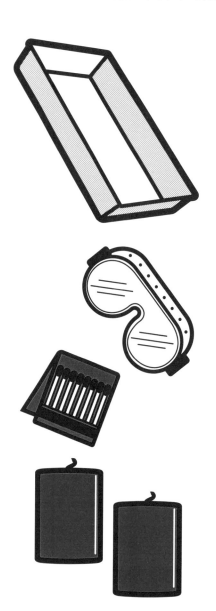

WHAT YOU NEED

2 small votive candles or tea lights
Matches
Baking pan
Safety goggles

HOW TO DO IT

1. Put on the safety goggles and place the candles in the pan.
2. Light the wicks with a match.
3. When the candles have burned down halfway, blow out the flame on one candle.
4. Let the other candle continue to burn until it goes out on its own. Where did the wax go?

WHAT'S GOING ON HERE?

Matter is neither created nor destroyed, a scientific principle known as the law of conservation of mass. When you light a wick, the flame creates heat, which melts the wax. As the wax heats, the molecules begin moving faster, turning it into a liquid. The liquid continues to be heated by the flame, causing the bonds in the molecules to break. The wax turns into a mixture of carbon dioxide and water vapor. The water evaporates and the gas mixes with the air around you. That is why there is little left of the second candle: The molecules are still around you, you just can't see them. When you blow out the flame before the candle wax is gone, the liquid wax begins to cool. The remaining molecules slow down and bond tightly, forming a solid again.

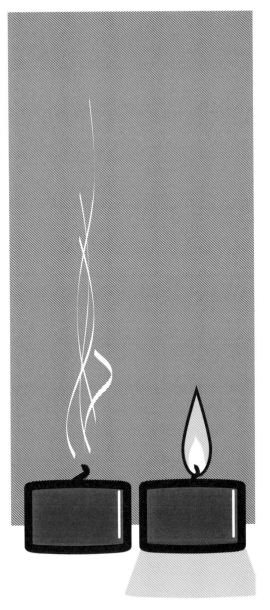

BURNING THE CANDLE AT BOTH ENDS

THERE'S AN OLD SAYING THAT SAYS IT'S BAD TO "BURN YOUR CANDLE AT BOTH ENDS." BUT WHY NOT GIVE IT A TRY?

WHAT YOU NEED

2 tall water glasses

7-inch taper candle

Knife or scissors

Ruler

Matches

3-inch steel nail

Butane lighter

Baking pan

Tape

HOW TO DO IT

1. Using the knife or scissors, carefully remove the wax from the bottom of the candle to reveal the wick. This will create a double-sided candle.

2. Use the ruler to find the exact center of the candle between the two wicks. Slowly push the nail through the wax at that middle point until it's sticking out of both sides. Tape the nail to the center of the candle to help hold it in place.

3. Place the water glasses side by side in the baking pan with about a 2-inch gap between them.
4. Place the candle in the center gap so that each end of the nail rests on a glass.
5. Light both ends of the candle.
6. Blow out the flames. What happens?

WHAT'S GOING ON HERE?

A principle of physics is that for every action there is an equal and opposite reaction. When the candle is lit, the wax begins to melt. Gravity causes the wax to drop, making that end of the candle lighter. So, it rises, pushing the other end of the candle lower. The process repeats with the other side until you blow out the flames and the wax stops melting from the heat.

RELIGHT DELIGHT

WHERE THERE'S SMOKE, THERE'S FIRE. SERIOUSLY.

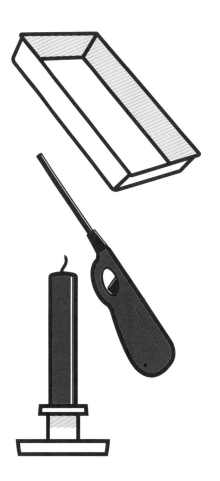

WHAT YOU NEED

Wax candle
Candlestick
Butane lighter
Baking pan

HOW TO DO IT

1. Place the candle firmly in the candlestick.
2. Have an adult light the wick on the candle. Wait 30 seconds or so, and then blow out the flame.
3. You'll see a trail of smoke rising from the wick. Immediately turn on the lighter and place the flame into the trail of smoke, about three inches above the candle. What happens?

WHAT'S GOING ON HERE?

Candles are made of a wax substance, which melts when exposed to heat. The wick is made of a flammable material, such as braided cotton. When the wick is lit, the flame causes the wax closest to it to vaporize, or turn into a gas. When you blow out the flame, some of the smoke still contains a small amount of material that was not completely burned. If you hold the flame in the trail of smoke, the unburned materials will reignite.

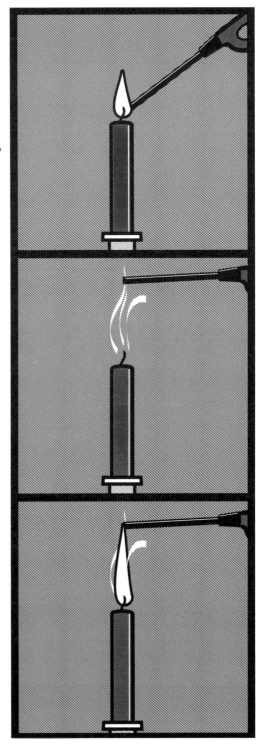

THE SECRET MESSAGE

WHAT WILL THE NEXT HOT SHOWER REVEAL ON YOUR BATHROOM MIRROR?

WHAT YOU NEED

Liquid soap
Water
Cotton swabs
Bathroom mirror

HOW TO DO IT

1. Squeeze a few drops of soap into a cup of water.
2. Mix well.
3. Dip a cotton swab into the liquid.
4. Write a message or draw a picture on the mirror.
5. Let the mirror dry.
6. When the next hot shower or bath fogs up the mirror, observe what happens.

WHAT'S GOING ON HERE?

Steam is made up of molecules of *water vapor*—water in gas form. The molecules are held together by electrical bonds. Soap molecules are attracted to the water molecules and break some of those bonds. This makes it hard for the water to stick to the mirror wherever you place the soap mixture.

THE POLLUTION DETECTOR

YOUR BATHROOM MAY SEEM CLEAN, BUT CAN YOU BE
SURE? WHAT GROSS STUFF MIGHT BE LURKING IN THAT
AIR YOU'RE BREATHING?

WHAT YOU NEED

White paper plate
Hole puncher
String or yarn
Shower rod or tape
Petroleum jelly
Magnifying glass

HOW TO DO IT

1. Punch a hole into the rim of the paper plate

2. Cut a piece of string about 12 inches long. Thread one end of the string through the hole in the plate. Tie a knot in the string.

3. Smear a thin coat of petroleum jelly onto the middle of the plate. Make sure you cover the center completely.

4. Tie the other end of the string to a curtain rod or shower rod. (If you don't have a curtain or shower rod, tape the string to the wall.)

5. Make sure the side with the petroleum jelly is facing out toward the bathroom.
6. Let this sit for a week. Check the surface each day.
7. How does the plate look after a week? What did it catch?
8. Try this experiment again in a different room. Or hang it from a tree and see what you catch outside!

WHAT'S GOING ON HERE?

All around you, tiny particles of dust and bacteria are floating through the air. Some of that dust is from pollution created outside your house. It's carried into the house on your clothes or shoes, or through the air vents. Some of it is the skin cells and hair you shed each day. Even the mold that grows on food starts as living spores that float in the air. Most of what is floating in the air isn't dangerous. But it's shocking to see what you catch with this pollution collector. You can sometimes see these particles in the narrow beams of sunlight that stream through a window. Otherwise, they're often too small to see with the naked eye.

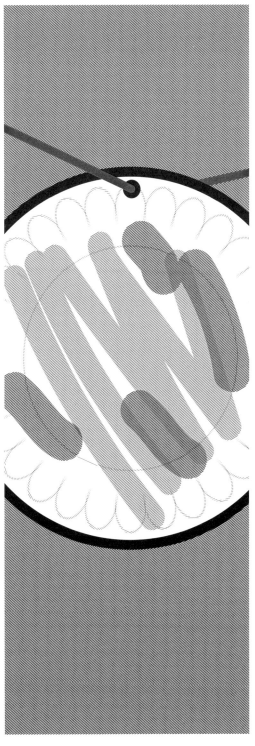

SO LONG, SCUM

EVER WONDER ABOUT THAT GUNK AROUND THE DRAIN OF THE TUB AFTER YOU TAKE A BATH? WANT TO MAKE SOME MORE?

WHAT YOU NEED

2 cups distilled water
Funnel
1 teaspoon Epsom salt
Two 2-liter soda bottles with caps
Liquid dish soap
Marker

HOW TO DO IT

1. Using the funnel, pour one cup of distilled water into each bottle.
2. Add the Epsom salt to one of the bottles. Let it dissolve.
3. Place a mark on the bottle so you can tell it apart from the other bottle.
4. Add three drops of liquid dish soap to each bottle.
5. Screw the caps on tightly and shake each bottle vigorously. Which bottle made more bubbles?

WHAT'S GOING ON HERE?

Tap water contains minerals. Some tap water contains more than others and people often refer to it as "hard water." When you add soap to hard water, a scum forms. That's part of what's clinging to your bathtub after you're done bathing. Distilled water is made by heating water and collecting the steam. This removes the minerals in the water. Water without minerals is sometimes called "soft water." People sometimes add water softeners to the water systems in their homes because they prefer soft water for bathing, cooking, and cleaning. That's also why people with hard water sometimes add liquid softeners to their laundry. Adding Epsom salt to distilled water introduces *magnesium sulfate*. This mineral reacts with the soap and interferes with the ability of the soap to clean. What's left over makes fewer, smaller bubbles.

THE INSTANT WATER FILTER

PREFER YOUR WATER TO BE CLEAN INSTEAD OF CHUNKY?
WELL, AREN'T YOU FANCY! HERE'S HOW TO DO IT.

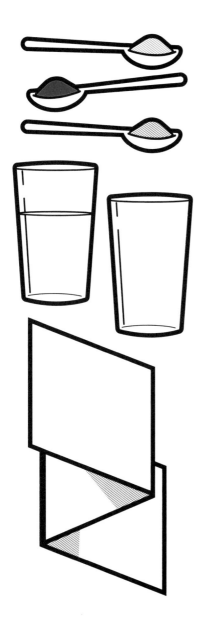

WHAT YOU NEED

Water
2 tall glasses
3–4 continuous sheets
   of paper towels
1/4 teaspoon each of 3 or 4 spices
Sink

HOW TO DO IT

1. Fill one glass halfway with tap water. Set the other, empty glass next to it.
2. Stir 1/4 teaspoon of a spice into the water.
3. Repeat with other spices until the water looks mucky and dirty.
4. Tear several sheets of paper towels from a roll, but keep them connected. Twist the paper towels until it forms a rope.
5. Put one end of the paper rope into the water. Let the other end hang over the empty glass.
5. Leave overnight and observe the next day.

WHAT'S GOING ON HERE?

Over time, water will travel up the rope and fall into the empty glass. The water transfer will stop when the water in each glass is equal. The solids will remain in the first glass. The natural wood fiber in the paper towels are a place for sticky water molecules to pull themselves along. As the first water molecules rise, they pull more water molecules with them. But the solids in the spices cannot travel up the rope. They remain behind, or stuck to the towel.

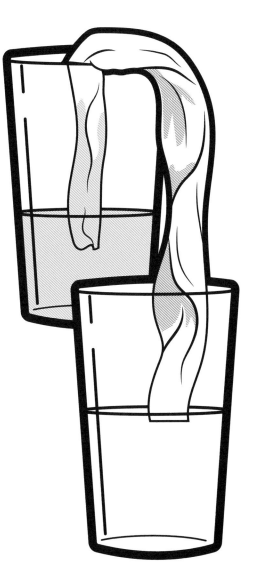

IT'S IRON, MAN

FOODS ARE OFTEN FORTIFIED WITH TRACE AMOUNTS OF METALS. HERE'S WHAT IT LOOKS LIKE WHEN YOUR STOMACH JUICES BREAK THEM DOWN. YUMMY!

WHAT YOU NEED

Magnet
1/4 cup iron-fortified wheat cereal
  (such as Total)
2 resealable plastic sandwich bags
Hammer
1 cup warm water
Spoon
Magnifying glass

HOW TO DO IT

1. Pour the cereal into the sandwich bag. Squeeze the air out of the bag and seal it.
2. Use your hands to break the cereal into the smallest pieces possible.
3. Open the bag and hold the magnet inside.
4. Close the bag again and gently crush the cereal with a hammer to make the pieces smaller. (This may result in small holes in the bag, but that's okay.)
5. Open the bag and pour the crushed cereal into the second sandwich bag. Add 1/2 cup of warm tap water.

6. Squeeze out the air and seal the bag.
7. Use your fingers to gently mix the cereal with the water until it begins to break down. If it becomes too thick, add more water. You want it to have the consistency of chicken soup.
8. Let it rest for 5 minutes. If there's air still in the bag, open a corner and gently squeeze it out, then reseal the bag.
9. Rub your magnet all over the bag. What happens? Do black particles start to appear?
10. Collect as many particles as you can, then lift the magnet about 1/8 inch above the bag. Move it around. Do the particles follow?
11. Put the magnet down and rub the bag again, collecting as many particles as possible.
12. Drag them to the corner of the bag. Can you lift the bag this way?

WHAT'S GOING ON HERE?

Iron is necessary to help your red blood cells carry oxygen to every part of your body. Are you surprised at how little there is? You don't need very much. But if you don't get enough, you become weak from the lack of oxygen in your blood, a disease called *anemia*.

A SHIRT TO TIE-DYE FOR

IT'S THE VERY HEIGHT OF BATHROOM FASHION.

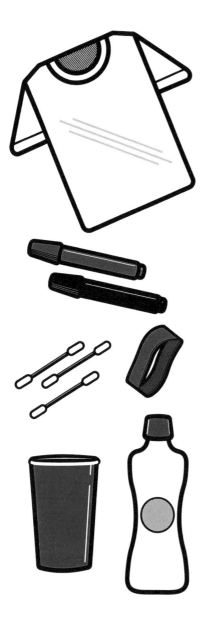

WHAT YOU NEED

Colored permanent markers
Rubbing alcohol
White cotton T-shirt
Plastic cup
Rubber band
Cotton swabs

HOW TO DO IT

1. Stretch part of the shirt over the plastic cup and hold it in place with a rubber band.
2. Draw a design on the shirt, leaving lots of white space between each color used.
3. Dip the cotton swab in alcohol. Touch the swab to one of the colors.
4. Let dry a few minutes.
5. Repeat steps 1-4 by tying other areas of the shirt to the cup, applying color, etc.
6. Let the shirt dry completely.
7. Tumble in a clothes dryer for 15 minutes to set the colors.

WHAT'S GOING ON HERE?

Marker ink dissolves in alcohol but not in water. The alcohol picks up the ink pigments as it spreads across the shirt. Once the alcohol evaporates, the ink will be left behind. Since this kind of ink doesn't dissolve in water, the shirt can be washed and the colored designs will remain.

OUT, OUT, SPOT!

FIGURING OUT HOW THE WASHING MACHINE MAKES STAINS DISAPPEAR WILL MAKE YOU GLAD YOU DON'T HAVE TO WASH YOUR CLOTHES BY HAND.

WHAT YOU NEED

Jar

Water

Spoon

Red and blue food coloring

Bleach

Eyedropper

Safety goggles

Rubber gloves

Apron

HOW TO DO IT

1. Bleach can damage eyes, skin, and clothes, so put on the goggles, gloves, and apron.
2. Fill the jar halfway with water. Add two drops of red food coloring. Stir until the color is evenly spread through the water.
3. Use the eyedropper to add a drop of bleach. Stir.
4. Add more bleach, one drop at a time, and stir.
5. Continue to add more drops until the color is much lighter. Let it sit for five minutes. What happened to the color?

6. Now add two drops of blue food coloring. Did it behave the same way as the red food coloring?
7. Let it sit five minutes. What happened?

WHAT'S GOING ON HERE?

Food coloring contains molecules that reflect specific wavelengths of light back to your eye. That molecule determines if you see red, blue, or some other color. Bleach contains a chemical known as *sodium hypochlorite*, which reacts with the dye molecules in the food coloring. The reaction breaks the molecular bonds in the dye, so it can no longer absorb or reflect light back to your eye. That makes the water look clear. The dye molecules are still there, however, suspended in the water. When you add the second color, it doesn't disperse or spread as well as the first color. If there's enough unused bleach still in the water, the blue color may slowly disappear as well. Now you know how laundry additives help remove color stains from your clothes: They just make them invisible!

RAISIN' THE RAISINS

NOW YOU CAN PLAY WITH YOUR FOOD IN THE BATHROOM.

WHAT YOU NEED

Seltzer
Tall water glass
6 small raisins

HOW TO DO IT

1. Fill the glass 3/4 full with seltzer.
2. Drop the six raisins into the glass.

WHAT'S GOING ON HERE?

When a solid such as a raisin is dropped into carbonated water, carbon dioxide gas is released. The gas clings to the dimpled surface of the raisin. The raisin is denser than the water, so it drops to the bottom when placed in the glass. Once the gas bubbles stick to it, the buoyancy increases, helping the raisins to float. At the top of the glass, the gas is able to escape, causing the raisins to drop to the bottom…and start the whole process again.

BATHROOM SLUSHY

SOMETIMES YOU JUST WANT TO KICK BACK WITH A COLD DRINK...IN THE BATHROOM.

WHAT YOU NEED

Resealable plastic sandwich bag
Glass jar with lid
Cold juice
1 teaspoon salt
1/2 cup water

HOW TO DO IT

1. Pour the water into the plastic bag and add the salt.
2. Squeeze air out of the bag before closing and freeze overnight.
3. Place the bag in the jar. Pour the cold juice in the jar and close it.
4. Shake extremely vigorously until the juice turns into slush. (It will take a couple of minutes.)

WHAT'S GOING ON HERE?

Ice forms when the temperature of water reaches 32 degrees Fahrenheit (0 degrees Celsius). When you mix salt with water, it lowers the freezing point of the water. In a standard freezer, for instance, the temperature of the salt/ice mixture can drop as low as -6 degrees Fahrenheit, so the ice stays cold longer. Because the cold juice is warmer than the ice, the heat transfers out of the juice. Ice made of salted water stays cold longer than regular ice, leaving time for the juice to transform into a slushy.

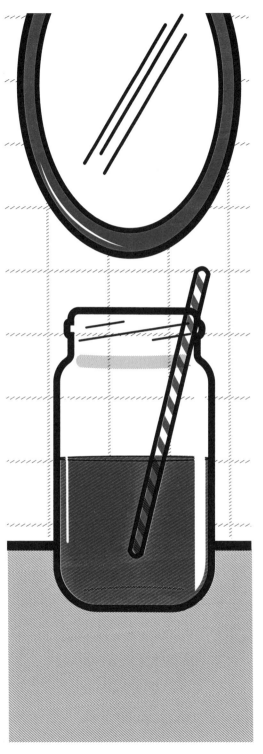

THE MAGICAL FINGER OF ICE

ONLY A WIZARD—OR MAYBE A BATHROOM SCIENTIST—CAN
FREEZE WATER WITH THE TOUCH OF A FINGER.

WHAT YOU NEED

Purified bottled water
  (not distilled)
Freezer
Water glass
Crushed ice

HOW TO DO IT

1. Place the bottled water in a freezer for about an hour. Lay it flat on its side. Don't shake it.
2. Remove the extremely cold (but not frozen) water and slowly pour into a glass, letting water flow down the side so it doesn't shake up.
3. Dip your finger in crushed ice.
4. Immediately dip the same finger into the cold water.

WHAT'S GOING ON HERE?

When water is frozen, it forms ice crystals. But these crystals form more easily when they form around a *contaminate*. Using purified water eliminates contaminates, which allows the water to remain in a very cold liquid state. Once the supercooled water touches a contaminant—your icy finger—a chain reaction occurs, with the water molecules packing together and spreading through the remaining liquid.

INSIDE JOB

MAKE ICE FORM INSIDE A CLOSED BOTTLE OF LIQUID WITH ONLY THE POWER OF YOUR MIND! (AND SCIENCE. SCIENCE PLAYS A BIG PART.)

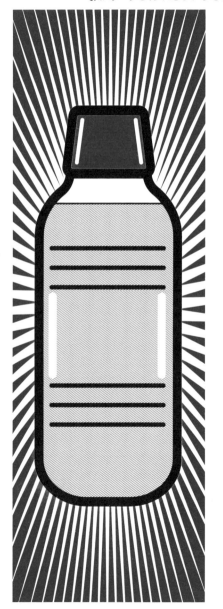

WHAT YOU NEED
Bottled distilled water
Freezer

HOW TO DO IT
1. Place the water in the freezer for 2–3 hours. Lay it flat. Don't shake it.
2. Carefully remove the bottle from the freezer without bumping it against anything.
3. Now, bang the bottle on a hard surface (nothing you can chip or break).

WHAT'S GOING ON HERE?
Water at room temperature is a liquid. Its molecules slide past each other, allowing it to flow. When water is frozen, ice crystals form. If you bang the bottle on a surface, it causes some of the molecules to line up in just the right way to form its own crystals. Those crystals are "seeds" that allow the remaining liquid to start a chain reaction and crystallize around them, causing the entire bottle to freeze.